Mometrix TEST PREPARATION

Praxis® II

Safety/Driver Education (0860) Exam Secrets Study Guide

DEAR FUTURE EXAM SUCCESS STORY

First of all, **THANK YOU** for purchasing Mometrix study materials!

Second, congratulations! You are one of the few determined test-takers who are committed to doing whatever it takes to excel on your exam. **You have come to the right place.** We developed these study materials with one goal in mind: to deliver you the information you need in a format that's concise and easy to use.

In addition to optimizing your guide for the content of the test, we've outlined our recommended steps for breaking down the preparation process into small, attainable goals so you can make sure you stay on track.

We've also analyzed the entire test-taking process, identifying the most common pitfalls and showing how you can overcome them and be ready for any curveball the test throws you.

Standardized testing is one of the biggest obstacles on your road to success, which only increases the importance of doing well in the high-pressure, high-stakes environment of test day. Your results on this test could have a significant impact on your future, and this guide provides the information and practical advice to help you achieve your full potential on test day.

Your success is our success

We would love to hear from you! If you would like to share the story of your exam success or if you have any questions or comments in regard to our products, please contact us at **800-673-8175** or **support@mometrix.com**.

Thanks again for your business and we wish you continued success!

Sincerely,
The Mometrix Test Preparation Team

Need more help? Check out our flashcards at:
http://mometrixflashcards.com/PraxisII

Written and edited by the Mometrix Exam Secrets Test Prep Team
Printed in the United States of America

Table of Contents

Introduction

Thank you for purchasing this resource! You have made the choice to prepare yourself for a test that could have a huge impact on your future, and this guide is designed to help you be fully ready for test day. Obviously, it's important to have a solid understanding of the test material, but you also need to be prepared for the unique environment and stressors of the test, so that you can perform to the best of your abilities.

For this purpose, the first section that appears in this guide is the **Secret Keys**. We've devoted countless hours to meticulously researching what works and what doesn't, and we've boiled down our findings to the five most impactful steps you can take to improve your performance on the test. We start at the beginning with study planning and move through the preparation process, all the way to the testing strategies that will help you get the most out of what you know when you're finally sitting in front of the test.

We recommend that you start preparing for your test as far in advance as possible. However, if you've bought this guide as a last-minute study resource and only have a few days before your test, we recommend that you skip over the first two Secret Keys since they address a long-term study plan.

If you struggle with **test anxiety**, we strongly encourage you to check out our recommendations for how you can overcome it. Test anxiety is a formidable foe, but it can be beaten, and we want to make sure you have the tools you need to defeat it.

Secret Key #1 – Plan Big, Study Small

There's a lot riding on your performance. If you want to ace this test, you're going to need to keep your skills sharp and the material fresh in your mind. You need a plan that lets you review everything you need to know while still fitting in your schedule. We'll break this strategy down into three categories.

Information Organization

Start with the information you already have: the official test outline. From this, you can make a complete list of all the concepts you need to cover before the test. Organize these concepts into groups that can be studied together, and create a list of any related vocabulary you need to learn so you can brush up on any difficult terms. You'll want to keep this vocabulary list handy once you actually start studying since you may need to add to it along the way.

Time Management

Once you have your set of study concepts, decide how to spread them out over the time you have left before the test. Break your study plan into small, clear goals so you have a manageable task for each day and know exactly what you're doing. Then just focus on one small step at a time. When you manage your time this way, you don't need to spend hours at a time studying. Studying a small block of content for a short period each day helps you retain information better and avoid stressing over how much you have left to do. You can relax knowing that you have a plan to cover everything in time. In order for this strategy to be effective though, you have to start studying early and stick to your schedule. Avoid the exhaustion and futility that comes from last-minute cramming!

Study Environment

The environment you study in has a big impact on your learning. Studying in a coffee shop, while probably more enjoyable, is not likely to be as fruitful as studying in a quiet room. It's important to keep distractions to a minimum. You're only planning to study for a short block of time, so make the most of it. Don't pause to check your phone or get up to find a snack. It's also important to **avoid multitasking**. Research has consistently shown that multitasking will make your studying dramatically less effective. Your study area should also be comfortable and well-lit so you don't have the distraction of straining your eyes or sitting on an uncomfortable chair.

The time of day you study is also important. You want to be rested and alert. Don't wait until just before bedtime. Study when you'll be most likely to comprehend and remember. Even better, if you know what time of day your test will be, set that time aside for study. That way your brain will be used to working on that subject at that specific time and you'll have a better chance of recalling information.

Finally, it can be helpful to team up with others who are studying for the same test. Your actual studying should be done in as isolated an environment as possible, but the work of organizing the information and setting up the study plan can be divided up. In between study sessions, you can discuss with your teammates the concepts that you're all studying and quiz each other on the details. Just be sure that your teammates are as serious about the test as you are. If you find that your study time is being replaced with social time, you might need to find a new team.

Secret Key #2 – Make Your Studying Count

You're devoting a lot of time and effort to preparing for this test, so you want to be absolutely certain it will pay off. This means doing more than just reading the content and hoping you can remember it on test day. It's important to make every minute of study count. There are two main areas you can focus on to make your studying count.

Retention

It doesn't matter how much time you study if you can't remember the material. You need to make sure you are retaining the concepts. To check your retention of the information you're learning, try recalling it at later times with minimal prompting. Try carrying around flashcards and glance at one or two from time to time or ask a friend who's also studying for the test to quiz you.

To enhance your retention, look for ways to put the information into practice so that you can apply it rather than simply recalling it. If you're using the information in practical ways, it will be much easier to remember. Similarly, it helps to solidify a concept in your mind if you're not only reading it to yourself but also explaining it to someone else. Ask a friend to let you teach them about a concept you're a little shaky on (or speak aloud to an imaginary audience if necessary). As you try to summarize, define, give examples, and answer your friend's questions, you'll understand the concepts better and they will stay with you longer. Finally, step back for a big picture view and ask yourself how each piece of information fits with the whole subject. When you link the different concepts together and see them working together as a whole, it's easier to remember the individual components.

Finally, practice showing your work on any multi-step problems, even if you're just studying. Writing out each step you take to solve a problem will help solidify the process in your mind, and you'll be more likely to remember it during the test.

Modality

Modality simply refers to the means or method by which you study. Choosing a study modality that fits your own individual learning style is crucial. No two people learn best in exactly the same way, so it's important to know your strengths and use them to your advantage.

For example, if you learn best by visualization, focus on visualizing a concept in your mind and draw an image or a diagram. Try color-coding your notes, illustrating them, or creating symbols that will trigger your mind to recall a learned concept. If you learn best by hearing or discussing information, find a study partner who learns the same way or read aloud to yourself. Think about how to put the information in your own words. Imagine that you are giving a lecture on the topic and record yourself so you can listen to it later.

For any learning style, flashcards can be helpful. Organize the information so you can take advantage of spare moments to review. Underline key words or phrases. Use different colors for different categories. Mnemonic devices (such as creating a short list in which every item starts with the same letter) can also help with retention. Find what works best for you and use it to store the information in your mind most effectively and easily.

Secret Key #3 – Practice the Right Way

Your success on test day depends not only on how many hours you put into preparing, but also on whether you prepared the right way. It's good to check along the way to see if your studying is paying off. One of the most effective ways to do this is by taking practice tests to evaluate your progress. Practice tests are useful because they show exactly where you need to improve. Every time you take a practice test, pay special attention to these three groups of questions:

- The questions you got wrong
- The questions you had to guess on, even if you guessed right
- The questions you found difficult or slow to work through

This will show you exactly what your weak areas are, and where you need to devote more study time. Ask yourself why each of these questions gave you trouble. Was it because you didn't understand the material? Was it because you didn't remember the vocabulary? Do you need more repetitions on this type of question to build speed and confidence? Dig into those questions and figure out how you can strengthen your weak areas as you go back to review the material.

Additionally, many practice tests have a section explaining the answer choices. It can be tempting to read the explanation and think that you now have a good understanding of the concept. However, an explanation likely only covers part of the question's broader context. Even if the explanation makes perfect sense, **go back and investigate** every concept related to the question until you're positive you have a thorough understanding.

As you go along, keep in mind that the practice test is just that: practice. Memorizing these questions and answers will not be very helpful on the actual test because it is unlikely to have any of the same exact questions. If you only know the right answers to the sample questions, you won't be prepared for the real thing. **Study the concepts** until you understand them fully, and then you'll be able to answer any question that shows up on the test.

It's important to wait on the practice tests until you're ready. If you take a test on your first day of study, you may be overwhelmed by the amount of material covered and how much you need to learn. Work up to it gradually.

On test day, you'll need to be prepared for answering questions, managing your time, and using the test-taking strategies you've learned. It's a lot to balance, like a mental marathon that will have a big impact on your future. Like training for a marathon, you'll need to start slowly and work your way up. When test day arrives, you'll be ready.

Start with the strategies you've read in the first two Secret Keys—plan your course and study in the way that works best for you. If you have time, consider using multiple study resources to get different approaches to the same concepts. It can be helpful to see difficult concepts from more than one angle. Then find a good source for practice tests. Many times, the test website will suggest potential study resources or provide sample tests.

Practice Test Strategy

If you're able to find at least three practice tests, we recommend this strategy:

Untimed and Open-Book Practice

Take the first test with no time constraints and with your notes and study guide handy. Take your time and focus on applying the strategies you've learned.

Timed and Open-Book Practice

Take the second practice test open-book as well, but set a timer and practice pacing yourself to finish in time.

Timed and Closed-Book Practice

Take any other practice tests as if it were test day. Set a timer and put away your study materials. Sit at a table or desk in a quiet room, imagine yourself at the testing center, and answer questions as quickly and accurately as possible.

Keep repeating timed and closed-book tests on a regular basis until you run out of practice tests or it's time for the actual test. Your mind will be ready for the schedule and stress of test day, and you'll be able to focus on recalling the material you've learned.

Secret Key #4 – Pace Yourself

Once you're fully prepared for the material on the test, your biggest challenge on test day will be managing your time. Just knowing that the clock is ticking can make you panic even if you have plenty of time left. Work on pacing yourself so you can build confidence against the time constraints of the exam. Pacing is a difficult skill to master, especially in a high-pressure environment, so **practice is vital**.

Set time expectations for your pace based on how much time is available. For example, if a section has 60 questions and the time limit is 30 minutes, you know you have to average 30 seconds or less per question in order to answer them all. Although 30 seconds is the hard limit, set 25 seconds per question as your goal, so you reserve extra time to spend on harder questions. When you budget extra time for the harder questions, you no longer have any reason to stress when those questions take longer to answer.

Don't let this time expectation distract you from working through the test at a calm, steady pace, but keep it in mind so you don't spend too much time on any one question. Recognize that taking extra time on one question you don't understand may keep you from answering two that you do understand later in the test. If your time limit for a question is up and you're still not sure of the answer, mark it and move on, and come back to it later if the time and the test format allow. If the testing format doesn't allow you to return to earlier questions, just make an educated guess; then put it out of your mind and move on.

On the easier questions, be careful not to rush. It may seem wise to hurry through them so you have more time for the challenging ones, but it's not worth missing one if you know the concept and just didn't take the time to read the question fully. Work efficiently but make sure you understand the question and have looked at all of the answer choices, since more than one may seem right at first.

Even if you're paying attention to the time, you may find yourself a little behind at some point. You should speed up to get back on track, but do so wisely. Don't panic; just take a few seconds less on each question until you're caught up. Don't guess without thinking, but do look through the answer choices and eliminate any you know are wrong. If you can get down to two choices, it is often worthwhile to guess from those. Once you've chosen an answer, move on and don't dwell on any that you skipped or had to hurry through. If a question was taking too long, chances are it was one of the harder ones, so you weren't as likely to get it right anyway.

On the other hand, if you find yourself getting ahead of schedule, it may be beneficial to slow down a little. The more quickly you work, the more likely you are to make a careless mistake that will affect your score. You've budgeted time for each question, so don't be afraid to spend that time. Practice an efficient but careful pace to get the most out of the time you have.

Secret Key #5 – Have a Plan for Guessing

When you're taking the test, you may find yourself stuck on a question. Some of the answer choices seem better than others, but you don't see the one answer choice that is obviously correct. What do you do?

The scenario described above is very common, yet most test takers have not effectively prepared for it. Developing and practicing a plan for guessing may be one of the single most effective uses of your time as you get ready for the exam.

In developing your plan for guessing, there are three questions to address:

- When should you start the guessing process?
- How should you narrow down the choices?
- Which answer should you choose?

When to Start the Guessing Process

Unless your plan for guessing is to select C every time (which, despite its merits, is not what we recommend), you need to leave yourself enough time to apply your answer elimination strategies. Since you have a limited amount of time for each question, that means that if you're going to give yourself the best shot at guessing correctly, you have to decide quickly whether or not you will guess.

Of course, the best-case scenario is that you don't have to guess at all, so first, see if you can answer the question based on your knowledge of the subject and basic reasoning skills. Focus on the key words in the question and try to jog your memory of related topics. Give yourself a chance to bring the knowledge to mind, but once you realize that you don't have (or you can't access) the knowledge you need to answer the question, it's time to start the guessing process.

It's almost always better to start the guessing process too early than too late. It only takes a few seconds to remember something and answer the question from knowledge. Carefully eliminating wrong answer choices takes longer. Plus, going through the process of eliminating answer choices can actually help jog your memory.

Summary: Start the guessing process as soon as you decide that you can't answer the question based on your knowledge.

How to Narrow Down the Choices

The next chapter in this book (**Test-Taking Strategies**) includes a wide range of strategies for how to approach questions and how to look for answer choices to eliminate. You will definitely want to read those carefully, practice them, and figure out which ones work best for you. Here though, we're going to address a mindset rather than a particular strategy.

Your odds of guessing an answer correctly depend on how many options you are choosing from.

Number of options left	5	4	3	2	1
Odds of guessing correctly	20%	25%	33%	50%	100%

You can see from this chart just how valuable it is to be able to eliminate incorrect answers and make an educated guess, but there are two things that many test takers do that cause them to miss out on the benefits of guessing:

- Accidentally eliminating the correct answer
- Selecting an answer based on an impression

We'll look at the first one here, and the second one in the next section.

To avoid accidentally eliminating the correct answer, we recommend a thought exercise called **the $5 challenge**. In this challenge, you only eliminate an answer choice from contention if you are willing to bet $5 on it being wrong. Why $5? Five dollars is a small but not insignificant amount of money. It's an amount you could afford to lose but wouldn't want to throw away. And while losing $5 once might not hurt too much, doing it twenty times will set you back $100. In the same way, each small decision you make—eliminating a choice here, guessing on a question there—won't by itself impact your score very much, but when you put them all together, they can make a big difference. By holding each answer choice elimination decision to a higher standard, you can reduce the risk of accidentally eliminating the correct answer.

The $5 challenge can also be applied in a positive sense: If you are willing to bet $5 that an answer choice *is* correct, go ahead and mark it as correct.

Summary: Only eliminate an answer choice if you are willing to bet $5 that it is wrong.

Which Answer to Choose

You're taking the test. You've run into a hard question and decided you'll have to guess. You've eliminated all the answer choices you're willing to bet $5 on. Now you have to pick an answer. Why do we even need to talk about this? Why can't you just pick whichever one you feel like when the time comes?

The answer to these questions is that if you don't come into the test with a plan, you'll rely on your impression to select an answer choice, and if you do that, you risk falling into a trap. The test writers know that everyone who takes their test will be guessing on some of the questions, so they intentionally write wrong answer choices to seem plausible. You still have to pick an answer though, and if the wrong answer choices are designed to look right, how can you ever be sure that you're not falling for their trap? The best solution we've found to this dilemma is to take the decision out of your hands entirely. Here is the process we recommend:

Once you've eliminated any choices that you are confident (willing to bet $5) are wrong, select the first remaining choice as your answer.

Whether you choose to select the first remaining choice, the second, or the last, the important thing is that you use some preselected standard. Using this approach guarantees that you will not be enticed into selecting an answer choice that looks right, because you are not basing your decision on how the answer choices look.

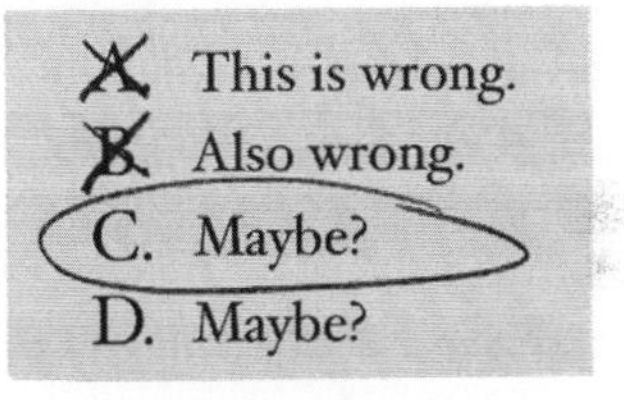

This is not meant to make you question your knowledge. Instead, it is to help you recognize the difference between your knowledge and your impressions. There's a huge difference between thinking an answer is right because of what you know, and thinking an answer is right because it looks or sounds like it should be right.

Summary: To ensure that your selection is appropriately random, make a predetermined selection from among all answer choices you have not eliminated.

Test-Taking Strategies

This section contains a list of test-taking strategies that you may find helpful as you work through the test. By taking what you know and applying logical thought, you can maximize your chances of answering any question correctly!

It is very important to realize that every question is different and every person is different: no single strategy will work on every question, and no single strategy will work for every person. That's why we've included all of them here, so you can try them out and determine which ones work best for different types of questions and which ones work best for you.

Question Strategies

☑ Read Carefully

Read the question and the answer choices carefully. Don't miss the question because you misread the terms. You have plenty of time to read each question thoroughly and make sure you understand what is being asked. Yet a happy medium must be attained, so don't waste too much time. You must read carefully and efficiently.

☑ Contextual Clues

Look for contextual clues. If the question includes a word you are not familiar with, look at the immediate context for some indication of what the word might mean. Contextual clues can often give you all the information you need to decipher the meaning of an unfamiliar word. Even if you can't determine the meaning, you may be able to narrow down the possibilities enough to make a solid guess at the answer to the question.

☑ Prefixes

If you're having trouble with a word in the question or answer choices, try dissecting it. Take advantage of every clue that the word might include. Prefixes can be a huge help. Usually, they allow you to determine a basic meaning. *Pre-* means before, *post-* means after, *pro-* is positive, *de-* is negative. From prefixes, you can get an idea of the general meaning of the word and try to put it into context.

☑ Hedge Words

Watch out for critical hedge words, such as *likely, may, can, often, almost, mostly, usually, generally, rarely*, and *sometimes*. Question writers insert these hedge phrases to cover every possibility. Often an answer choice will be wrong simply because it leaves no room for exception. Be on guard for answer choices that have definitive words such as *exactly* and *always*.

☑ Switchback Words

Stay alert for *switchbacks*. These are the words and phrases frequently used to alert you to shifts in thought. The most common switchback words are *but, although*, and *however*. Others include *nevertheless, on the other hand, even though, while, in spite of, despite*, and *regardless of*. Switchback words are important to catch because they can change the direction of the question or an answer choice.

⊘ Face Value

When in doubt, use common sense. Accept the situation in the problem at face value. Don't read too much into it. These problems will not require you to make wild assumptions. If you have to go beyond creativity and warp time or space in order to have an answer choice fit the question, then you should move on and consider the other answer choices. These are normal problems rooted in reality. The applicable relationship or explanation may not be readily apparent, but it is there for you to figure out. Use your common sense to interpret anything that isn't clear.

Answer Choice Strategies

⊘ Answer Selection

The most thorough way to pick an answer choice is to identify and eliminate wrong answers until only one is left, then confirm it is the correct answer. Sometimes an answer choice may immediately seem right, but be careful. The test writers will usually put more than one reasonable answer choice on each question, so take a second to read all of them and make sure that the other choices are not equally obvious. As long as you have time left, it is better to read every answer choice than to pick the first one that looks right without checking the others.

⊘ Answer Choice Families

An answer choice family consists of two (in rare cases, three) answer choices that are very similar in construction and cannot all be true at the same time. If you see two answer choices that are direct opposites or parallels, one of them is usually the correct answer. For instance, if one answer choice says that quantity x increases and another either says that quantity x decreases (opposite) or says that quantity y increases (parallel), then those answer choices would fall into the same family. An answer choice that doesn't match the construction of the answer choice family is more likely to be incorrect. Most questions will not have answer choice families, but when they do appear, you should be prepared to recognize them.

⊘ Eliminate Answers

Eliminate answer choices as soon as you realize they are wrong, but make sure you consider all possibilities. If you are eliminating answer choices and realize that the last one you are left with is also wrong, don't panic. Start over and consider each choice again. There may be something you missed the first time that you will realize on the second pass.

⊘ Avoid Fact Traps

Don't be distracted by an answer choice that is factually true but doesn't answer the question. You are looking for the choice that answers the question. Stay focused on what the question is asking for so you don't accidentally pick an answer that is true but incorrect. Always go back to the question and make sure the answer choice you've selected actually answers the question and is not merely a true statement.

⊘ Extreme Statements

In general, you should avoid answers that put forth extreme actions as standard practice or proclaim controversial ideas as established fact. An answer choice that states the "process should be used in certain situations, if..." is much more likely to be correct than one that states the "process should be discontinued completely." The first is a calm rational statement and doesn't even make a definitive, uncompromising stance, using a hedge word *if* to provide wiggle room, whereas the second choice is far more extreme.

⊘ BENCHMARK

As you read through the answer choices and you come across one that seems to answer the question well, mentally select that answer choice. This is not your final answer, but it's the one that will help you evaluate the other answer choices. The one that you selected is your benchmark or standard for judging each of the other answer choices. Every other answer choice must be compared to your benchmark. That choice is correct until proven otherwise by another answer choice beating it. If you find a better answer, then that one becomes your new benchmark. Once you've decided that no other choice answers the question as well as your benchmark, you have your final answer.

⊘ PREDICT THE ANSWER

Before you even start looking at the answer choices, it is often best to try to predict the answer. When you come up with the answer on your own, it is easier to avoid distractions and traps because you will know exactly what to look for. The right answer choice is unlikely to be word-for-word what you came up with, but it should be a close match. Even if you are confident that you have the right answer, you should still take the time to read each option before moving on.

General Strategies

⊘ TOUGH QUESTIONS

If you are stumped on a problem or it appears too hard or too difficult, don't waste time. Move on! Remember though, if you can quickly check for obviously incorrect answer choices, your chances of guessing correctly are greatly improved. Before you completely give up, at least try to knock out a couple of possible answers. Eliminate what you can and then guess at the remaining answer choices before moving on.

⊘ CHECK YOUR WORK

Since you will probably not know every term listed and the answer to every question, it is important that you get credit for the ones that you do know. Don't miss any questions through careless mistakes. If at all possible, try to take a second to look back over your answer selection and make sure you've selected the correct answer choice and haven't made a costly careless mistake (such as marking an answer choice that you didn't mean to mark). This quick double check should more than pay for itself in caught mistakes for the time it costs.

⊘ PACE YOURSELF

It's easy to be overwhelmed when you're looking at a page full of questions; your mind is confused and full of random thoughts, and the clock is ticking down faster than you would like. Calm down and maintain the pace that you have set for yourself. Especially as you get down to the last few minutes of the test, don't let the small numbers on the clock make you panic. As long as you are on track by monitoring your pace, you are guaranteed to have time for each question.

⊘ DON'T RUSH

It is very easy to make errors when you are in a hurry. Maintaining a fast pace in answering questions is pointless if it makes you miss questions that you would have gotten right otherwise. Test writers like to include distracting information and wrong answers that seem right. Taking a little extra time to avoid careless mistakes can make all the difference in your test score. Find a pace that allows you to be confident in the answers that you select.

⊘ KEEP MOVING

Panicking will not help you pass the test, so do your best to stay calm and keep moving. Taking deep breaths and going through the answer elimination steps you practiced can help to break through a stress barrier and keep your pace.

Final Notes

The combination of a solid foundation of content knowledge and the confidence that comes from practicing your plan for applying that knowledge is the key to maximizing your performance on test day. As your foundation of content knowledge is built up and strengthened, you'll find that the strategies included in this chapter become more and more effective in helping you quickly sift through the distractions and traps of the test to isolate the correct answer.

Now that you're preparing to move forward into the test content chapters of this book, be sure to keep your goal in mind. As you read, think about how you will be able to apply this information on the test. If you've already seen sample questions for the test and you have an idea of the question format and style, try to come up with questions of your own that you can answer based on what you're reading. This will give you valuable practice applying your knowledge in the same ways you can expect to on test day.

Good luck and good studying!

Safety and Driver Education Curriculum

PRIMARY RESPONSIBILITIES

The number one responsibility of any driver is safety. You must make driving decisions that will ensure the safety of you, your passengers, people in other vehicles, and pedestrians. You should also do your best to never damage anyone's property. However, if you must choose between injuring a person and damaging property, property damage is the obvious choice. Being a safe driver requires you be cooperative with other drivers and to drive defensively. Stay alert. Observe the other drivers around you. Try to determine what decisions other drivers will make, and react accordingly. Once you have made a decision, follow through with it—sudden changes in direction or speed due to indecision can create dangerous situations.

DUI, DWI, OUI, OWI

All of these terms refer to citations for driving a motor vehicle while under the influence of alcohol or an intoxicant. These are the four most common terms, but some states may use unique terms other than these.

- DUI: Driving Under the Influence. Most often a DUI refers to driving while over the legal limit for blood alcohol level. It can also refer to driving under the influence of drugs. This is the most common police term for drunk driving.
- DWI: Driving While Intoxicated or Driving While Impaired. This is also commonly used for driving under the influence of drugs, alcohol, or other controlled substances.
- OUI: Operating a vehicle Under the Influence
- OWI: Operating a vehicle While Intoxicated

ALCOHOL

Drinking and driving creates a dangerous situation that results in thousands of deaths every year. When you drink, the reaction of alcohol within your body affects your brain, specifically the areas that control your judgment and motor skills. When under the influence of alcohol you are more likely to make dangerous decisions that you wouldn't normally make. You might decide to race off a stop or to speed, for example. Alcohol also affects your reflexes. When you are driving under the influence of alcohol, your reaction time will be slower and you will be less alert. This makes it more likely that you will not stop in time for a light or for a braking vehicle or that you will not be as aware of the vehicles around you. Alcohol impairs every aspect of your driving skills, making you dangerous to those in the vehicle with you and to the people in the vehicles around you.

For legal adults, each state has a blood alcohol limit that determines whether or not it is legal for someone who has been drinking to drive. In most states this limit is .08. While this limit establishes a legal guideline, some drivers may be impaired at a lower blood alcohol level. Many physiological factors determine how alcohol affects any given individual. Body weight, the number of drinks and the period of time over which they were consumed, alcohol tolerance, and gender all affect how you will react to alcohol. The average adult can consume one drink an hour and not be considered impaired. However, it is always safest not to drink at all if you plan to drive.

Underage drivers should not drink any alcohol at all if they plan to drive.

Many states have an open container law that prevents alcohol being accessible in a vehicle while driving. Most open container laws state that no person in a moving vehicle will actively consume alcohol. They also state that containers containing alcohol will not be present in the passenger area of the vehicle if the seal on the container has been broken. It is against open container laws to put alcohol into a different container that is labeled as non-alcoholic or to change the label on an alcohol bottle. In some states, open container laws are stricter than in others. Be certain you know the laws of the state you are driving in.

There are many ways you can attend a social gathering, have a good time, and still get home safely. If you are attending the setting with friends, choose one of you as the designated driver. That person will agree not to drink alcohol at all during the course of the event and will drive the other people home. Take turns being the designated driver at different events.

If a designated driver is unavailable, plan to use public transportation to get home safely. Either the bus or a cab is a safe way to travel when you've been drinking.

If neither of these plans is practical, make arrangements to stay the night either at the location of the social event or at a hotel that is within walking distance.

If you drink and drive, you may be arrested. If you are pulled over while driving under the influence of alcohol, the police officer may request a blood alcohol test or a Breathalyzer test to find out your blood alcohol levels. Most states have an "implied consent" law that means you must take these tests if the officer requests it. Depending on whether or not it is a first offence, your license will be revoked for a period of time ranging between months and years. You may also be fined thousands of dollars. You may be sentenced to jail time. If you are involved in an accident while under the influence of alcohol, the penalties will be worse.

Over-the-counter drugs

Many over-the-counter drugs like aspirin or ibuprofen do not affect your driving ability if you use them correctly. However, several over-the-counter medicines can adversely affect your driving abilities. These include cold medications that contain antihistamines or diet pills that contain stimulants. Antihistamines can make you drowsy, impairing your reaction time and putting you in danger of falling asleep at the wheel. Stimulants can make you fell jumpy and impair your judgment. They can also lead to an energy crash that makes you feel fatigued. It is important to always check the warning labels on over-the-counter drugs before taking them if you plan to drive.

Impaired driving

There are many ways you can compromise your driving ability that do not involve drugs or alcohol. Driving while tired or angry puts you at greater risk for an accident. Fatigue may lead to slow reaction times. Anger may lead to poor judgment or aggressive driving.

Attempting to multitask while driving also impairs your skills by taking your full attention off the road. Some activities to avoid while driving include talking on a cell phone, applying make up, eating, or reading a map. Some drivers even attempt to change clothes while driving. Any one of these activities will be better accomplished by pulling over, completing the activity and then resuming driving when you are done. Often people resort to multitasking while driving because they did not give themselves enough time to reach their destination. Always allow extra time for your travels.

Heart Disease, Epilepsy, Diabetes

Heart Disease: A condition that puts the sufferer at greater risk for heart attack and fainting. Heart disease is one of the most common diseases in our society. Events such as heart attack or fainting can be triggered by stress. Stress do to poor driving conditions or a near accident can cause a driver suffering from heart disease to become incapacitated, which is likely to result in an accident.

Epilepsy: A brain disorder that causes seizures or convulsions. Most epileptic patients are under a doctor's care and take regular medication to prevent seizures. In these circumstances, they present little danger on the road.

Diabetes: A condition where the sufferer's body is unable to properly process blood sugar. Treatment may require insulin medication. Diabetics must be conscious of when they are at higher risk to an insulin reaction or high or low blood sugar extremes. Both can cause blackouts or erratic behavior. High-risk times include periods when a doctor is adjusting insulin dosages or when a sufferer skips a meal.

Emotions

Different emotions can have an impact on your judgment, your ability to pay attention, your alertness, or other important factors that influence driving. For example, driving when you are angry will make you more susceptible to road rage. Driving while you are sad or depressed may make you less alert. Driving while tired can slow your reaction times.

If you are angry, you should delay driving until you have calmed down. Try natural stress reducing strategies like a brisk walk or sitting quietly and breathing deeply. Make sure you are in control of your emotions before you decide to drive.

If you are depressed or anxious, try an activity that will keep your mind off your emotional state while driving, but that won't distract you from driving. For instance, you might listen to a book on tape, sing to yourself, or note how many different state license plates you see while on the road.

If you are tired, rest before driving or ask someone else to drive.

Road Rage

Road rage is when a driver reacts in anger to another driver's mistake or inconsiderate behavior. Because a driver acting out of rage has a vehicle weighing thousands of pounds at his disposal, he can quickly create a very dangerous situation.

To avoid acting out in rage, allow yourself plenty of time to get where you are going. Also, decide ahead of time that you won't allow other drivers to make you angry. Commit to immediately forgiving any other drivers' rude decisions or mistakes.

If you find yourself a target of road rage, try to remove yourself from the situation. Avoid making eye contact. Don't make any hand gestures that could be misunderstood. Slow down or pull onto a different road. If an angry driver follows you, proceed to a public place. Call the police if you feel threatened.

Road rage is always dangerous. It causes drivers to make poor decisions or pay inadequate attention to the road. There are three different kinds of road rage. Quiet road rage involves complaining, letting impatience drive you to poor decisions, and driving competitively. This kind of road rage takes your full attention off the road. Verbal road rage involves shouting, using intimidating body language directed at other drivers, and honking inappropriately. This kind of road rage creates the same dangers as quiet road rage, but it also antagonizes other drivers, which can compound the dangers. Finally, there is epic road rage, where an angry driver may deliberately try to put another car in danger or follow a driver with the intention of fighting him or her. This kind of road rage often warrants involving the police.

Drivers who suffer from road rage usually drive too fast. They often ignore posted signs, making it difficult to predict their actions. They may cruise in the passing lane or change lanes suddenly without signaling. If you identify a driver participating in these kinds of behaviors do not respond with your own road rage. Instead, slow down and remove yourself from the vicinity of the problem driver. Remember at all times that you share the road with other drivers. Be ready to immediately forgive other drivers' errors. And always drive courteously.

Aggressive or Defensive Driving

Aggressive Driving: Driving in a reckless manner. Aggressive driving usually involves speeding, accelerating quickly off a start and waiting longer than is safe to brake. It can also involve following other vehicles too closely, switching lanes suddenly or weaving traffic. Aggressive driving puts you and drivers around you in danger and at higher risk for incidents of road rage.

Defensive Driving: Driving in a manner that is alert and aware and that involves prudent decisions. A defensive driver tries to reduce the risks of accidents before they ever occur. The defensive driver will follow at a proper distance, accelerate and brake in a slow steady manner, obey speed limits and maintain constant awareness of his or her surroundings.

Motor Oil

Proper maintenance of a vehicle will help to maintain the vehicle's optimum gas mileage. The motor oil you use affects gas mileage. Check your vehicle handbook to determine the best motor oil for your car, and then use that grade of motor oil. Using a different grade of motor oil than recommended by your vehicle's manufacturer can reduce gas mileage by up to 2%.

Regularly changing your motor oil is another important step to keeping your car's fuel efficiency up. In most vehicle's, the motor oil should be changed every three months or every three thousand miles. Some vehicles have a different maintenance schedule. Check the operator's manual for details.

Reducing Gas Usage

Of increasing concern is gas consumption. The following are ways to conserve:

- Obeying the speed limit is the best way to conserve gasoline as you drive. Most cars function optimally when cruising at 55 to 65 miles per hour. Fuel economy decreases when you drive faster or change speeds often.
- Aggressive acceleration is another fuel waster. Accelerate at a steady, smooth rate unless safety demands otherwise.
- Most cars are equipped with cruise control and/or overdrive gears. Cruise control helps you to maintain a constant freeway speed and reduces gas usage. Using an overdrive gear at freeway speeds also improves gas mileage.
- Reducing the weight in your vehicle will improve gas mileage. Don't leave heavy, unnecessary items in the trunk when you drive. Reduce the time you allow your car to save even more gas.
- A well-functioning engine improves a vehicle's gas mileage. Engines work hard when you drive. They have lots of parts that experience wear-and-tear, and they use fluids that breakdown over time. When these elements aren't functioning as well as they could be, your gas mileage begins to suffer. By getting regular tune ups, you'll ensure that your spark plugs and brakes are in good working order and that your transmission is working properly. All of these things can impact your gas mileage. By regularly maintaining your vehicle according to the manufacturer's recommended schedule, you will use less gas and improve the vehicle's performance, as well.

- Proper tire maintenance is important for safety, performance, and getting the best possible gas mileage. Tires that are low in air decrease your car's fuel efficiency. Tires that are out of alignment also lower the gas mileage and can cause the vehicle to pull in one direction or another making it less safe to drive. Finally tires that have worn-down tread also create unsafe driving conditions. You can ensure better gas mileage and safer driving conditions by regularly checking the air in your tires and keeping them inflated to the recommended pressure, by having your wheels aligned on a regular schedule and by replacing tires before they become too worn.
- Keeping your engine tuned and your tires in good repair are two well-known steps to better gas mileage, but don't overlook the role of your car's air filter. A clogged air filter will actually take a greater toll on your gas mileage than poorly inflated tires. By simply switching out your old, clogged air filter for a new one, you can immediately improve gas mileage by as much as 10%. The reason is that your car's engine requires airflow to function optimally. Reduced airflow means reduced efficiency. The air filter also prevents impurities from reaching the engine where they can do damage. A clean air filter is an important component to good car maintenance and for maintaining good fuel efficiency.
- When buying a car, the decision you make will impact your gas usage, possibly for years to come. Rather than buying an inefficient vehicle, consider one that will help to conserve gas. Smaller cars generally use less fuel than larger cars. The lower weight and smaller engine improve gas mileage. There are also many fuel-efficient vehicles available. Some get more than 40 miles per gallon. Hybrid vehicles are another option and can afford you an additional tax deduction to offset extra costs. Also consider cars that make it possible to use alternative sources of fuel, such as bio-diesel or electricity.

Highway System

The highway transportation system consists of three parts: people, vehicles, and roadways. As a driver, you are part of this system. First, you must be aware of your responsibility to yourself, the people riding with you, the people traveling in other vehicles near you, and people in your vicinity but not within vehicles. They are all part of the highway system and your decisions can affect their safety. The vehicles on the roads are the next part of the system. These include other cars, large trucks, motorcycles, and in some areas even farm equipment. You must be knowledgeable of any special considerations you need to give specific kinds of vehicles. Finally, the roads that you drive on are the final component. Different roads require different driving considerations. Driving on a two-lane state highway requires more caution that driving on a divided freeway, for example.

Rules of Basic Safety

To drive safely you must make sure all passengers and yourself wear their seatbelts. This is important even if you are traveling only a short distance. An accident can happen at any time and seatbelts can reduce injuries in a collision. You must pay particular attention that children are properly secured with child safety belts for two reasons. First, children are more likely to create a distraction if they are moving about within the vehicle. Second, children are more likely to be injured in an accident if they are not properly belted in. To drive safely, you must also make sure that you give driving your full focus. Do not drive while under the influence of drugs or alcohol. Don't drive when you are tired. Don't introduce distractions while you are driving. For example, wait until you can pull over and stop to use your cell phone. Finally, you must be aware of all vehicles and pedestrians in your vicinity and take precautions not to endanger them.

Seatbelt Safety

Everyone within a vehicle should wear a safety belt. In many states, safety belts are mandated by law. In the front seat, safety belts can prevent deadly injuries, especially when working in conjunction with air bags. For children under 16, the back seat is safer than the front seat. Most states have child safety laws specifying how children must be secured. These laws may vary by state. In general, they are determined by age, height, and/or weight. Infants should ride in a rear-facing child safety seat. Toddlers should ride in a child safety seat with a five-point harness system. Young children can use a car's standard seatbelts, but may require a booster seat to make those restraints safe and effective.

Peripheral Vision

When driving you use all aspects of your vision. It is important to be aware of not only what is in front of your vehicle but also behind you and to both sides. Your peripheral vision—seeing out of the corner of your eye—helps you to notice vehicles or obstacles on either side of you (pedestrians or cyclists, for example). Even while you are looking forward, you should still be aware of movements and objects that are at your side. You cannot give these objects your direct focus without taking your eyes from the road ahead. Instead use your side mirrors and quick glances to the side to maintain awareness of objects in your vicinity.

Judging Distance and Speed

Being able to judge distance and speed when driving is important for safe stopping, merging and passing. Even in the clearest of conditions, some people have a difficult time accurately judging the distance and speeds of objects around them. One way to practice is to observe the three-second rule. Pick a stationary object along side the road. Note as the car ahead of your vehicle passes it. Begin counting slowly by seconds until you pass the same object. The number you reach is how many seconds you are behind the vehicle.

In addition to this exercise, the best way to build your skill at judging speeds and distances is simply to observe. Pay attention to how quickly a vehicle in the oncoming lane reaches you, to how quickly you reach objects in the distance, and to how much distance it takes to safely pass vehicles at varying speeds.

Braking Considerations

The number one consideration to stopping a car safely is the distance between you and the vehicle or object ahead of you. Following at a safe distance that allows you adequate time to recognize the need to stop and come to a complete stop before a collision is the best way to ensure safe braking. Road conditions must also be considered. Allow more distance between yourself and other vehicles in wet or slick conditions, as your vehicle will require more distance to come to a complete stop. You must also know whether your vehicle uses antilock brakes or not. In a vehicle with antilock brakes you can apply steady, hard pressure to the brake when you need to stop quickly. Without, antilock brakes you may have to pump the brake in order to avoid a skid.

Space Between Vehicles

At regular road speeds it is safe to follow two to three seconds behind a vehicle. At highway speeds it is safer to allow four seconds. The following are three common situations when you should allow for more space between you and the vehicle ahead of you.

- When roads are slippery, you will need more time to stop your vehicle. Allow extra distance between you and the car ahead of you to allow ample time to react and stop should it be necessary.

- When the car behind you wishes to pass you, it is courteous and safer to slow down and make room between you and the vehicle in front of you. This makes it so the passing driver will be able to move safely back into the proper lane.
- When visibility is poor due to fog, rain, or the nighttime, it is prudent to follow more distantly and allow for more stopping time.

Emergency Vehicles

These vehicles require more space to maneuver and may be required to act in unpredictable ways. Allow at least 500 feet when following an emergency vehicle.

Large Vehicles with Limited Backward Visibility

Drivers of trucks, buses and campers cannot see you if you follow them too closely. A rule of thumb is that you should be able to see their side-view mirrors. That means they can see you. Following at a distance will also improve your view of the road ahead.

Motorcycles

If a motorcycle tips over, the driver is a great risk of being run over and seriously injured. By increasing your following distance, you can help to minimize the chance you will hit the motorcycle driver should he lose control.

Maintaining Adequate Side Space

Maintaining a safe space on either side of your vehicle makes safe turning and safe lane changes possible. Driving to the side of large vehicles on multi-lane roads is dangerous. Semi-trucks, buses, and campers all have a large blind spot to the side. You create a hazard by maintaining a steady speed in their blind spot. Either speed up or slow down so that you are in front of or behind that vehicle. Use caution when passing bicyclists, emergency vehicles, or people walking. Give them as much space as you safely can. Be mindful of parked vehicles as people may exit them or step out from between them. Whenever possible, you should pull into the inside lane to allow extra space in these situations.

Seat and Mirror Positioning

As the driver, you need to be able to see clearly in all directions. This means making sure your seat and mirrors are properly positioned. You should be sitting high enough to see the road before you clearly. If your vehicle has a driver side air bag, you want your seat height positioned so the air bag will deploy against your chest rather than your face. You also need to be able to comfortably reach the accelerator and brake pedals. If necessary, sit on a cushion to make certain you are at the proper height. Adjust the rear-view mirror so that it gives you a clear view out the back window. You should be able to just glance at the mirror, moving nothing but your eyes, to see the road behind. Position your side view mirrors so that they show you the road behind you and the lane to the side. You should not have to do more than lean forward a little to use your side view mirrors.

Making Turns

Right turns are made from the right-hand lane of the road you are on into the right-hand lane of the road you are entering. Be careful not to cross into the lane next to you on the road you are starting from. Do not change lanes on the road you are entering until you have completed your turn.

Left turns are made either from the left-most lane or from the left-hand turn lane if one is available. When turning left, turn into the innermost lane (the left lane) of the road you are entering. In some controlled intersections multiple lanes will turn left. If this is the case be careful to turn into the proper lane. As with right turns, be cautious not to cross into any other lanes, and do not change lanes until you have completed your turn.

4-WAY INTERSECTIONS

When approaching a 4-way intersection that is not controlled by either a traffic signal or stop signs, slow down. If you are the first to reach the intersection you have the right-of-way, and may proceed through the intersection. If another car reaches the intersection first that driver has the right-of-way. If two cars reach an intersection simultaneously, yield right-of-way to the driver on the right. If four cars reach an intersection simultaneously from all four directions, use caution and courtesy to determine who goes first. After the first car moves through the intersection, the next car to move through should be the one to the right of the first car, and so on until all the cars have moved through the intersection.

SAFE PARKING

When parking your vehicle, always move as far out of traffic as you can. (Do not stop or park on freeways or highways. If your vehicle becomes disabled, pull as far onto the shoulder as possible.) If there is a curb, park your vehicle as close to it as possible. If there is a space marked off for parking, use it. Once you've parked, put your transmission into gear if it is a manual. For automatic transmissions, use the "park" gear. Do not leave your key in the ignition or the engine running. Check for traffic before exiting the vehicle. When you park, make sure you choose a place that will not obstruct visibility for other drivers. For example, do not park too close to a corner on the right hand side as you approach an intersection as it may prevent other drivers from seeing cross traffic.

If you park on a hill facing upwards place the vehicle in gear (any gear for a manual transmission, "park" for an automatic). Set the parking brake. Then turn the car's wheels away from the curb. If the car should start to roll, it will roll into the curb, which will halt its progress.

If you park facing downhill, follow the same procedure, but turn your wheels toward the curb. Again, should the vehicle roll, it will roll into the curb.

If there is no curb, turn your wheels toward the edge of the road whether you are facing uphill or downhill. Should your vehicle begin to roll, it will roll out of the flow of traffic.

ROUNDABOUTS

A roundabout is a traffic control device that requires approaching vehicles either to stop before entering or to yield to vehicles already within the roundabout. Drivers must progress around a circular structure in order to turn or to continue straight ahead. There are four entrances and exits to a standard roundabout. To turn right, you will exit at the first exit past where you enter; to go straight you'll use the second exit; to turn left you'll use the third exit.

When approaching a roundabout, slow down. Do not enter the roundabout until there is a space in the existing traffic. Drive around the structure until you reach the exit you wish to use. If you miss your exit, you can continue around the structure until you reach it again.

PROHIBITED PARKING PLACES

There are more than a dozen places where parking is restricted or prohibited. These include intersections, sidewalks, crosswalks, and construction areas. You also should not park closer than 30 feet to a controlled intersection. You should not park within 20 feet of a crosswalk. Allow 15 feet between your vehicle and a fire hydrant when parking, and 50 feet between your vehicle and a railroad crossing. Do not park within 20 feet of a fire station driveway (allow 75 feet on the side of the road opposite the driveway). Do not park on railroad tracks, bridges, overpasses, or freeways.

Do not park more than 12 inches from a curb. Allow at least five feet between your vehicle and driveway or alley entrances. Do not park where signs are displaced prohibiting parking. These guidelines may vary by state.

Gripping the Steering Wheel

To effectively control the steering wheel (and the vehicle), you need to use two hands. You should place your hands on opposite sides of the steering wheel. The shorter distance between your hands should take up about one third of the wheel. Different driving instructors recommend different positions. If you look at the steering wheel like it is a clock, a 10-and-2 hand placement is a common recommendation. Positioning your hands between the eight and nine on the left and between the three and four on the right is another safe grip. This grip allows you to make gentle turns without having to release the steering wheel. Both grips will keep your hands clear of the airbag.

For sharp turns, lift one hand over the other on the steering wheel, so that one hand always remains firmly gripping the wheel. When you bring the wheel back to a straight-ahead position, don't allow it to slide back to that position. Bring it there manually. This ensures you maintain control.

Avoiding Speeding

In many situations, it is difficult to judge your speed. This is especially true if you have gone from a high-speed roadway to a much slower-rated road. In these situations, it is very easy to speed. The best way to avoid speeding is to regularly check your speedometer, and adjust your speed as necessary. To avoid speeding, you must also remain aware of the speed limit. Note posted speeds, and follow them. They are there to make the roads safer for everyone. Each state also has standard speeds for different roads or zones. Unless there is a sign that states otherwise, you must obey the standard speed. Find out the standard speeds for school zones, city streets, highways, and interstates in your area.

Scanning

Safe driving depends on the driver being able to see well. As the driver, you must maintain constant awareness of your surroundings to the front, sides and back of the vehicle. You do this by scanning the road around your vehicle. A few times each minute, you should sweep the area around your car with your eyes, taking note of potential hazards. Scanning the road in front of you is important. It will help you avoid sudden stops or collisions with bicyclists, pedestrians, parked vehicles, or vehicles entering the road. You also need to be aware of what is coming so that you can avoid sudden stops. You should always be aware of the road up to ten seconds ahead. In a city setting, this means scanning a block ahead. On a highway, you should scan a quarter mile ahead.

Scanning the road at least ten seconds ahead (one city block in town, a quarter mile on the highway) provides benefits beyond safety. Sudden braking and unnecessary acceleration both use more fuel than steady speeds and gradual slowing do. By scanning ahead, you can usually avoid the need to brake or stop suddenly. When you see possible hazards before the become hazards, you can react earlier. By reacting earlier, your reaction will often be less drastic, which does improve your gas mileage.

Scanning ahead also helps preserve the flow of traffic. Sudden braking can create a domino affect that reaches many cars behind you. It can slow the flow of traffic significantly.

Intersections

Intersection: Any place where traffic crosses or enters a roadway. Intersections include side streets and driveways.

When entering traffic from a driveway, stop first. Make sure there is a safe gap in the cross traffic for you to pull into or move across. Check to the sides for bicyclists or pedestrians. When the way is clear move into the flow of traffic.

When approaching an intersection of two roadways, look both right and left for vehicles, bicyclists and pedestrians. If the intersection is clear, proceed through. Continue to look right and left for any oncoming cross traffic. Only move through an intersection if you will be able to move all the way through it. Do not block at intersection by stopping midway through.

Making Turns

Before making a turn, you need to begin signaling 100 feet ahead of time. You must slow down to a safe turning speed. If you are turning left, you must wait for a gap in the oncoming traffic that is wide enough for you to safely move through. You must check the road you are turning into for obstacles and for pedestrians, bicyclists, and other vehicles. Finally, if you are turning left, you must look again at the oncoming traffic and make certain it is still safe to proceed.

At controlled intersections, always look for pedestrians or vehicles that are going against their light. You won't expect them to be there, but not all drivers and pedestrians obey posted traffic signals. Remain aware.

Crossing Railroad Tracks

Slow your speed when approaching train tracks. Look in both directions along the track to be certain no train is approaching. If there is a bend in the tracks or your view is otherwise obstructed, establish quiet in your vehicle (turn off your radio, turn off the air condition, ask passengers to be quiet), and roll down the window to check if you can hear an approaching train. This is particularly important if the train crossing in question does not have warning signals.

Do not enter the train tracks unless you can cross them complete. Do not stop on the tracks. If there is more than one train track, make sure you can safely cross all of them before proceeding.

Changing Lanes

When you want to move from your lane into the lane next to you, the first step is to signal your intent. Turn on your turn signal in the direction you plan to move. Check your review mirror for vehicles already in the lane you are moving into. If they are coming up fast, wait until they pass you. Check your side mirror for any vehicles to the side of you. Next, turn your head to glance into your blind spot—this is the area at the rear quarter panel of your vehicle. You can't see this area in your mirrors; you will have to turn your head to check it. Do so quickly. Do not take your eyes off the road ahead of you for more than an instant. If there is a lane on the far side of the one you plan to enter, check to make sure no one is changing lanes from there. If all checks show you have a clear space, proceed to change lanes.

Backing Up

Backing up is one of the least safe motions in a vehicle. It is necessary sometimes. To increase your safety level when reversing, make sure you physically check behind your vehicle. This is most important before you back out of a driveway. Children's toys or children themselves may be out of sight of your rear view mirror. Turn and look directly out the back windshield. You will have better visibility than if you rely solely on your side view and rear view mirror. Move slowly. Steering is more difficult in reverse; going slowly will give you better control. Frequently check to the left and right for oncoming traffic or for pedestrians. Yield to anyone approaching.

Headlights and High Beams

Your headlights help you to see at night. They also make it easier for you to be seen by other drivers. For safety, you must use your headlights at all times between a half an hour after sunset and a half an hour before sunrise.

You must also use your headlights any time visibility is compromised. In the fog, in the snow or rain, or if there is smoke or dust clouding the road--these are all situations where you should use your headlights.

Your headlights have a high setting. When the road is clear of other vehicles, your high beams will increase your visibility. Do not use your high beams if you are following within 300 feet of a vehicle or if you are within 500 feet of an oncoming vehicle.

Using the Horn

A vehicle's horn is there to get the attention of drivers that may be entering or creating a dangerous situation. You should only use your horn as a warning. Use a short blast of the horn as a warning when danger is not imminent. You might this to warn a pedestrian or bicyclist that is inadvertently entering your lane or to get the attention of a vehicle that you don't think has seen you. Use a stronger blast if there is immediate danger. You might honk loudly at someone about to run into the street or at another vehicle that is about to hit you. Do not use your horn because you are impatient. Honking at someone who is slow off a stop is not appropriate. It is also inappropriate to honk at another driver out of irritation.

Proper Hand Signals

Communication with the other drivers around you is a crucial element of safe driving. In some circumstances, your turn signals or brake lights may not be working or may not be visible. In these situations, you are still responsible for conveying your intentions to the drivers around you. You can do so with hand signals. Roll down your window and use your left arm to signal. To signal a left turn or a lane change moving left, extend your arm straight out of the window. To signal a right turn or a lane change moving right, extend your arm out the window but bend at the elbow. Your forearm should be at a right angle to your upper arm with the hand extend up. To signal your intention to slow down or stop, extend your arm out the window and bend the forearm down at the elbow.

The Basic Rule

The basic rule of driving states that you must drive at a speed that is appropriate and safe for the conditions you are in. This means that you could be going the speed limit and still be ticketed for speeding if road conditions demand that you slow down.

While it is never legal to drive over the posted speed limit, the basic rule makes you as the driver responsible for determine what speed is safe. If you are driving in inclement weather or heavy traffic conditions, you must adjust your speed downward. To not do so may create unsafe conditions and put you and the vehicles around you at risk.

Adjusting Speed

Determining whether you need to slow down and travel at a speed under the posted limit is left to your discretion. Some obvious situations mandate a slower speed.

Slippery roads either from ice, snow or rain make it more difficult to stop. You should travel at a slower speed that allows you to react to things in plenty of time to come to a complete, controlled stop. Wet roads are at their slickest just after a first rain.

Curvy roads will require you to adjust your speed with each curve. Slow down before entering a curve so that your vehicle doesn't skid or lose control.

Heavy traffic means you need to adjust your speed to move with the flow of traffic. Attempting to weave between cars in an effort to move faster than the traffic around you is reckless.

Freeway Merging

To merge with high-speed traffic on an interstate, enter the freeway ramp and begin accelerating. You should reach freeway speeds by the end of the ramp. Turn on your signal to communicate your intent to move into the closest lane. Look for a safely sized gap between two vehicles for you to move into. Ideally you want to have enough room to leave at least two seconds between you and the vehicle in front of you and another two seconds between you and the vehicle behind you. You may have to adjust your speed to time your entry onto the freeway. Do not come to a stop on the ramp. If you realize you won't have a space to merge into at the speed you are at, slow down and then speed up to merge when it is safe.

Stopping Times Factors

When you drive your safety and the safety of those around depends on your ability to stop before a collision occurs. The amount of time it takes you to stops varies with your speed. Traveling at 30 mph, it can take 200 feet to react to a hazard and come to a complete and safe stop. At 50 mph, that stopping distance doubles. (For perspective, 200 feet is about one half of a city block.) If your visibility is less than 400 feet, it becomes unsafe to travel at 50 mph—you won't be able to stop in time if you need to make a sudden, unexpected stop. If raining, foggy conditions, at night, or when your view is obstructed by hills or curves, you need to adjust your speed to match the amount of distance you have to stop. If you can only see 200 feet in front of you, you should not travel at speeds greater than 30 mph.

Generally, it takes four full seconds to react to a hazard, apply the brakes, and come to a full stop. You can use the four-second rule to determine if you are traveling at a safe speed or if you should slow down. Pick a stationary object at the side of the road that is at the limit of your visibility. Begin counting by seconds until you pass that object. If you pass it less than four seconds, you are driving to fast to be able to stop safely. You should slow down. At night, your headlights illuminate the road approximately 400 feet in front of you, but this distance can vary. Use the four-second rule to make certain you are not driving too fast at night, too.

Passing a Vehicle

First, be sure you are in a section of the road where it is legal for you to pass. You should have either a single dashed yellow line dividing you and the oncoming traffic or a double-yellow line a dashed line closet to you.

Next make sure you have ample room to pass. If you are traveling 55 mph, it will take you on average 10 seconds and 800 feet to pass a vehicle. To do so safely, there must be at least 1600 feet between you and any oncoming traffic. That's about one third of a mile or four city blocks. Gauging the speed of an oncoming car can be difficult. If you are uncertain, wait for a better opportunity.

When passing, signal your intent to move into the oncoming lane. Accelerate steadily to pass the vehicle. Then signal to move back into the flow of traffic. It is safest to only pass one vehicle at a time. You should not have to speed to pass.

AVOIDING COLLISIONS

Whenever you are faced with the possibility of a collision, you can attempt to avoid it in three different ways. First, you can adjust your speed. You may be able to accelerate out of the way of a vehicle coming from the side or you may be able to slow down and avoid colliding with a car stopping suddenly. Second, you can change directions. You may need to swerve to avoid a collision. Be careful that you can swerve safely. You do not want to avoid one collision by causing another. You may be able to avoid a hazard by changing lanes. Finally, you can attempt to communicate with the drivers around. You may turn your flashing yellow lights on to alert the car behind you to a problem and avoid being rear-ended. You may honk your horn to gain the attention of a danger. Even hand signals and eye contact may help you work with the drivers around you to avoid a dangerous situation.

PLANNING FOR LONG TRIPS

If you plan to take a long trip requiring you to drive for several hours, there are a number of steps you can take to ensure your safety during the trip. First, one week before you leave have your vehicle serviced if it is due. Change the oil. Have the tires rotated. If the wheels need aligning, have that done before you leave. Just before you leave, check over the vehicle. Make sure no warning lights are coming on and staying on. Check the tire pressure. Also check weather reports and road conditions. Give your itinerary to a family member who is not traveling with you. Make sure you plan plenty of time for your trip including rest breaks. Also pack any maps or directions that you need.

SYMPTOMS OF FATIGUE

You can recognize if you are becoming fatigued by the symptoms. Fatigue goes beyond merely feeling tired. There are four main symptoms of fatigue. If you find it difficult to keep your attention on any one thing for any length of time, you may be suffering fatigue. If you cannot remember things that would normal be easy for you to remember that is another sign of fatigue. Fatigue can also make it difficult for you to make decisions quickly. Finally, if you find you are having a hard time understanding new ideas, then you may be fatigued. If you become fatigued while driving, let someone else drive or pull over and rest.

PARALLEL PARKING

Parallel parking means parking your vehicle so it is parallel with the curb. When no other vehicles are parked along the curb, signal your intent to pull over to the curb, and then slowly maneuver your vehicle alongside the curb. If you are parallel parking between two parked vehicles, turn on your right turn signal. Pull alongside the vehicle parked in front of the space you wish to park in and stop. Put your car into reverse and slowly back into the space. Next, put your car into drive and slowly correct the angle of the car, so that it is parallel to the curb and not at an angle. You may have to do a series of corrections, switching between reverse and drive. Maintain awareness of traffic coming up behind you throughout the entire process of parking.

TAILGATERS

If another driver begins to follow you too closely, do not react with anger. Do not brake suddenly to startle them. Doing so could cause them to rear end you. Instead, let up slightly on your accelerator and increase the space between you and the next vehicle in front of you. Pull your car to the right side of the lane you are in. Communicate with the driver behind you by signaling well ahead of any turns or lane changes you plan to make. If the driver continues to tailgate you, attempt to remove yourself and your vehicle from the situation. Either change lanes to allow the tailgater to pass, or pull of the road when it is safe to do so.

Crossing the Centerline

As a rule, you should never cross the centerline dividing you from oncoming traffic. There are times when a driver coming towards you may cross that line. You must be prepared. There are ways to recognize when this is a potential danger. If there is an obstruction narrowing the oncoming lane, a bus or truck making a wide right turn, or a double-parked vehicle and oncoming car may have to cross the centerline to avoid the obstruction. These situations are the easiest predict. Some are more difficult to anticipate. A driver may swerve into your lane to avoid a sudden movement from another car, because of vehicle failure, or because they are driving under the influence of a controlled substance. Always be alert to the actions of oncoming traffic so that you give yourself time to react if they enter your lane.

In the event that an oncoming car crosses the center lane, the first thing you should do is slow down. Move as far to the right of your lane as you safely can. If there are multiple lanes traveling in your direction, move from the left lane into one that is farther to the right. If changing lanes is not an option, attempt to gain that driver's attention. Turn on your headlights. If your headlights are already on, flash them. Sound your horn. If these methods don't cause the driver to correct his error, you may need to take measures to evade the oncoming vehicle. Search for an open space to the right that you can swerve into if it becomes necessary.

Executing a Curve

Curves often have a posted suggested speed that is lower than the enforced speed limit. Gradual curves may have a suggested speed of 25 mph up to the regular posted speed limit. Sharp curves will have a suggested speed lower than 25 mph. Slow to the recommended speed as you approach curve. Be careful to stay in your lane and you round the curve. Watch the road as far into the curve as you can—curves reduce visibility, so be ready to react quickly if there is an unexpected hazard in the road. When you are half way through the curve, gradual speed up and begin steering out of the curve.

Accidentally Leaving the Road

Long drives or driving while fatigued puts you at higher risks for driving errors. One common error is to gradually drift to one side of the road or the other. If you drift right, and your right tires leave the road, you must know how to react in order to recover. If there is a significant difference between the materials of the road and the materials your right tires are on, this can make the vehicle more difficult to control. Remove your foot from the accelerator, but resist the urge to use your brake—it may cause you to lose control. Hold tightly to the steering wheel. Check if it safe to move back into the right lane of the road. Gradually move the steering wheel to the left, and then straighten out as you re-enter traffic.

Exiting a Freeway

When you exit a freeway, you want to be careful that you don't disrupt the flow of traffic by slowing down to soon. Communicate your intent to leave the freeway by using your signal at least 300 feet before the exit. Check your mirrors, and look into your blind spot before moving into the exit lane. Do not begin braking while you are still on the freeway. Instead reduce the pressure of your foot on the accelerator pedal. Use the white line at the right of the road to guide you off the freeway onto the exit ramp. Once you are one the exit ramp begin braking and follow any suggested speed postings.

Brake System

The braking system on your vehicle is what gives you the ability to stop. Obviously, if this system is not functioning properly, it creates a great driving hazard. The braking system in simplified form includes the brake pedal, a master cylinder, brake lines, and disc and drum brakes that actually stop the wheels using friction. The braking system is designed to leverage the amount of force you apply with your foot, multiplying it so that it is enough to stop the entire vehicle. If any component of the brake system breaks down, your stopping ability becomes compromised. Because braking systems are based on friction, it is natural that the components become worn over time. Any time your brakes feel spongy or soft, cause the car to shake during stopping, give off a funny smell, make a squealing noise, or that the brake pedal loses its tension, take your vehicle into a mechanic for service.

Vehicle's Exterior Lights

Vehicles have five sets of lights that help you to communicate with other drivers and see at night. These lights are the headlights, brake lights, turn signals, reverse lights, and tail lights.

The headlights and taillights allow you to see and be seen when driving at night. The turn signals blink on the right or left side of the car to signal vehicles around you that you plan to turn or change lanes. Brake lights are at the back of the car and signal vehicles behind you that you are applying the brakes and are slowing down or stopping. Your reverse lights are small white lights at the back of your vehicle that signal you are in a reverse gear and may be backing up.

Damaged Windshield or Wipers

Your windshield provides your visibility when driving. If your view becomes obstructed, you become a less safe driver. Damaged or crack windshields can obstruct visibility. They also are more likely to break if you are involved in an accident or if your windshield is struck by debris. You should arrange for cracked or extensively chipped windshields to be fixed or replaced. Your windshield wipers keep your windshield clear during inclement weather. Wiper blades become worn over time and can result in reduced visibility. Replacing wiper blades is an easy task that most drivers can do on their own. Most automobile stores carry a variety of wiper blades that you can purchase as replacements.

Steering System

Most vehicles now have power steering. This hydraulic system consists of the steering wheel and a hydraulic pump that leverages the force of your turning action, making it easier to turn the vehicle. The engine drives the hydraulic pump.

Another less common power steering system is an electric version. This kind of system uses a computer module to respond to torque on the steering wheel. A small electric motor then applies force to the wheels during a turn. Electric power steering systems improve gas mileage.

Steering system problems are easy to identify. If you notice a sudden or gradual change in the ease with which you can turn or if you have to turn the wheel a ways before the vehicle responds, then take your car in and have a mechanic check the steering system.

Suspension System

The suspension system on a car helps make the vehicle easier to control. It also offers some protection to the vehicle by absorbing the force of bumps in the road. The suspension helps maintain your vehicle's ground clearance and proper wheel alignment, too.

A modern suspension system uses a series of shock absorbers, springs and struts. The springs help to insulate the body of your vehicle from the bumps in the road while still allowing your tires to maintain full contact with the road. The struts and shock absorbers help limit the amount the springs bounce when the vehicle hits a bump. All components of your suspension system are subject to wear and tear. If you notice you feel more movement in your vehicle on bumpy roads or that you have more difficulty controlling the vehicle over bumps, have a mechanic look at your suspension system.

Exhaust System

A vehicle's exhaust system does three things. It discharges the waste products left over from the fuel burning process within the engine. It reduces the noise of the engine's waste discharge. The exhaust system also breaks down dangerous pollutants into their less harmful components.

The efficient removal of waste products from the engine is important to the engine's performance. If fuel waste begins to build up within the engine, it can damage the engine, decreasing its efficiency and eventually leading to the need for major repairs.

Noise reduction is important. The engine's discharge is under high pressure and very loud. The exhaust system uses a muffler to significantly reduce the noise of the engine.

The exhaust system uses a catalytic converter to break down dangerous compounds, making an engine give off less pollution.

An engine produces many dangerous gases as part of its combustion process. These gases include hydrocarbons and carbon monoxide. Carbon monoxide is particularly dangerous. It is colorless and odorless. If you breathe significant amounts in during a prolonged period of time, it can cause you to fall asleep and even die. Part of the exhaust system's function is to discharge dangerous fuel wastes outside of the vehicle. A leak in the exhaust system can result in carbon monoxide building up within the vehicle's passenger area, which can result in the death of the people in the vehicle. Because not all exhaust leaks show obvious symptoms, you should have the exhaust system checked periodically. Having it looked at during the vehicle's yearly tune-up is a smart plan.

Poorly Maintained Engine

The engine is like the heart of a vehicle. If it is in poor condition many different problems can result. A neglected engine may run with less power than it was designed to. This can create a hazardous driving situation if you need to accelerate quickly to avoid a collision, for example. A poorly running engine will produce more pollutants making the car dirtier to drive. The vehicle will not get optimum gas mileage if the engine is in poor repair. In extreme cases, a neglected engine may fail to start or it may stop working while you are driving. A stalled car in the flow of traffic creates an immediate road hazard.

When Brakes Fail

Brake failures create a particular hazard on the road. If you press your brake pedal and it doesn't respond, it may have lost pressure because of a leak in the line. Begin pumping the brake pedal. This action may help to build enough pressure in the brake system to bring you safely to a stop.

If pumping the pedal fails, engage the emergency brake. Do so slowly or you risk putting the card into a skid. If your vehicle does begin to skid, release the emergency brake. If you have a manual transmission, you can slow your vehicle by shifting into successively lower gears. Look for a place along the road to coast your vehicle to a stop.

TIRE BLOWOUTS

If you should experience a tire blowout while driving, it is a natural reaction to slam on your brakes. However doing so will cause you to lose control of your vehicle. You must resist that reaction. Instead, take your foot off the gas pedal, and concentrate on keeping the car pointed straight ahead. With a blown tire, your car will pull sharply in the direction of the blowout. It will be more difficult to steer than usual. Hold the steering wheel tightly, straighten out your vehicle, and then keep it going straight. Now, lightly use your brake pedal. Push it in and release it. This will help you slow down more without causing you to lose control. Gently steer your vehicle onto the road's shoulder as you come to a complete stop.

LOSING POWER WHILE DRIVING

If your engine loses power while you are driving, remain calm. Steer the car to the side of the road and then stop safely out of the path of traffic. You will need to keep in mind that most modern vehicles have power steering and power brakes. Both of these systems may depend on the engine for their power, making it harder to turn and harder to stop if the engine power has failed. Recognize that both systems still work, but you will need to use more force. Grip the steering tightly and turn with a firm, steady pressure. With your foot, push very hard on the brake pedal in order stop.

WHEN HEADLIGHTS FAIL

If you are driving at a time when your headlights are required for safety and your headlights fail, you must take immediate action to preserve your safety and the safety of other drivers. First, try turning your headlights off and on several times. Sometimes, this can make them come back on. If that does not work, turn on your emergency flashers so that other drivers can see you and will be aware that you have a problem. If your vehicle is equipped with fog lights, turn those one. Exit the road as soon as you safely can. Do not drive again until conditions permit you to drive without headlights or until your headlights are working again.

STUCK GAS PEDAL

In some cases, the accelerator pedal can become stuck in a depressed position. This will rev the engine higher and higher, and make your vehicle gain speed. In this situation, carefully watch the road, so that you can anticipate any upcoming hazards and avoid them. Immediately shift the vehicle into neutral, so that you won't continue to gain speed. Begin searching for a safe place to exit the road and pull over as soon as you are able to. Once you are out of the flow of traffic, turn off the engine.

ENGINE OVERHEATING

Your engine uses water to keep it from overheating. The temperature gauge on your dashboard tells you the temperature of the water. If the gauge needle enters the red area, it indicates that your vehicle is overheating.

In the event of your engine getting too hot, find a safe place to pull over and turn off the car as well as everything that may be drawing power from the engine (lights, radio, air condition, etc.) Leave your key in position, so you can turn on the car's heater even with the engine off. The heater bleeds heat from the engine, so turning it helps the engine cool. If your engine continues overheating, call a tow truck.

Do not attempt to check the water levels in your radiator until your car has ample time to cool. Opening the radiator while it is hot can lead to injury.

Oil Light

Your engine requires oil to run well. If it does not have oil to lubricate the hot, fast-moving parts within the engine, the engine may seize and expensive damage is the result. Your car is equipped with an oil gauge that lights up if the oil pressure falls below a certain level. If your oil light comes on, you should immediately pull over and turn off the engine. Call a tow truck to move your car to a mechanic's shop, as the problem must be fixed before you can safely drive again.

You can help prevent oil leaks and other problems in your car by having your oil changed regularly. Every 3 months or every 3000 miles is a general guideline, but check your operator's manual for the best maintenance schedule for your car.

Electrical System Gauge

Many systems in your vehicle require electricity to run. Electricity is supplied through the battery. If your battery light (also known as the electrical system gauge) comes on, this indicates there is a problem with the electrical system in your vehicle. In most cases, your car will still run, but you may find you have difficulty starting it and may require a jumpstart. (It's a good idea to keep jumper cables in your car for situations such as this one.) When your battery light comes on, schedule a visit to your mechanic to have the system checked out and repaired. Otherwise, you run the risk of becoming stranded.

Jumpstarting a Vehicle

If your vehicle has a dead battery, you may be able to recharge with the help of a running vehicle. Turn both vehicles off. Using jumper cables, attach one red clamp to the positive node on the dead battery. Attach the other red clamp to the positive node on the battery of the assisting vehicle. Next attach the nearest black clamp to the negative node on the assisting vehicle's battery. Attach the other black clamp to the engine block of the dead vehicle. (This is safer than attaching it to the dead battery.) Turn on the engine of the assisting car. Sometimes, you will be able to start the dead vehicle right away. Sometimes it will take a few minutes. Keep the cars connected for a few minutes. When you're ready detach the negative cables and then the positive cables. Do not turn the newly charged car off for at least 20 minutes, so that the battery has a chance to fully recharge as you drive.

Panel Lights and Gauges

Fuel Gauge: This gauge tells you how much fuel you have left in your tank. As a general guideline, you should add gas to your tank whenever it falls to a quarter full. Most fuel gauges are accompanied by a low fuel warning light. When this comes on, you are low on fuel and should refuel as soon as possible.

High Beam Indicator: This light tells you that you have your bright lights on. Remember to turn your headlights down when traffic is approaching or if you are following another vehicle.

Seatbelt Warning Light: Most cars have a seatbelt warning light that comes on when you turn the vehicle on reminding you to use your seatbelt.

Anti-lock Brake System Light: If this light comes on and stays on, there may be a problem with your anti-lock brakes. The standard brakes will function, but schedule a mechanic's visit to have the system checked. If the additional brake warning light is on, do not drive.

NECESSARY SYSTEM CHECKS

Before driving, check around your vehicle to make sure there are no obstacles you might back over. (This is especially important if you will be backing out of a driveway.) Once in the vehicle, fasten your seatbelt. Next adjust your seat. You should be able to comfortable see out the windshield and easily reach the control pedals. Once, your seat is in position, adjust your mirrors. You should be able to see directly out the back window with a just a glance at your rearview mirror. You should be able to see to the side and behind you with your side view mirrors. Have a clear view to all sides of your vehicle is very important.

STARTING THE ENGINE

Once you have checked around your vehicle, adjusted your seat, and positioned your mirrors, you can start your vehicle's engine. Leave the parking brake on until you are ready to move. Put the vehicle into Park for an automatic or neutral for a manual. Keeping your foot on the brake pedal, turn the key to the on position. Check your gauges to make sure there are not any problems. Now turn the key to the Start position in the ignition. One the engine starts up, you can let go of the key. Check your gauges one more time to make sure everything is still functioning properly before you begin driving.

TIRES

TIRE CONSTRUCTION

Differently constructed tires serve different purposes. All tires have essentially the same basic components. The bead bundle sits at the wheel rim. It is enforced with steel and makes it possible for a tire to endure the forces of driving without slipping out of place. The body and sidewall make up the bulk of the tire. Layers of fiber make up the body. The sidewall gives the tire additional stability. Finally, the tread is the part of the tire that meets the road. It's made of rubber.

The main variables in tires are whether they are radial (most tires produced today are) or made with a diagonal bias or a bias belted construction. In a radial construction, the body layers are perpendicular to the tire's tread. A diagonal bias tire has piles that run at a diagonal to the tread.

Different tire tread patterns serve different purposes. All season tires work for most purposes. Some tires are treaded to prevent hydroplaning. Others are treaded for extra traction in the snow.

The side of a tire carries a series of several different numbers and letters that provide information about the tire's construction. The first letter indicates the type of vehicle the tire is intended for. 'P' means passenger; "LT" means light truck; "T" means temporary and denotes a spare tire. The next number is the tire width measured in millimeters. The next number is height of the tire given as a percentage of the width. It's commonly called the aspect ratio. The next letter in the series tells you the tire's construction: R for radial, D for diagonal, and B for bias belted. The final number is the rim width in inches. This number tells you what rim size the tire was made for.

TIRE PRESSURE

A standard tire pressure gauge looks a like a silver pen. It has a round head on one end, and a sliding scale on the other. The air within your tire exerts a constant pressure on the tire. The more air you put into a tire, the greater the pressure will become. Proper tire pressure is important to a car's performance. Use a tire pressure gauge to periodically measure the pressure in your tires and add air if needed.

To measure the pressure, locate the valve on your tire. Remove the cover if it has one. Take the round head of the pressure gauge, and line the open side up with the tire valve. Cover the tire valve and press downwards for a moment. Doing so will release air against the pressure gauge. The sliding scale will be forced out according to the pressure from the air. You can then read the scale to determine the pressure within your tire. (The recommended pressure will be listed on the tire's exterior.)

Choosing Tires

When choosing a tire, make certain you choose the correct size and load-bearing capacity for your vehicle. Also, check the tire's speed rating. The speed rating indicates how well the tire deals with heat from driving at faster speeds for long periods. If you do a lot of highway driving or regularly make longer trips, than a tire with a higher speed rating will last longer for you. The three most common speed ratings are S, T, and H. S is a lower rating better for driving around town. H is a higher rating and will endure longer when faced with regular freeway driving.

The final consideration to make is the traction of your tire. Some tires are designed to perform well in wet weather conditions, some in snow and ice, and others for driving on dry roads. Consider the weather patterns where you live before choosing a tire. If you live a region that gets snow in winter, consider all-season tires in summer and snow tires in winter.

Rotating Tires

Rotating a car's tires makes the tires wear more evenly. This increases fuel efficiency, lowers road noise, and makes the tires last longer.

On a front wheel drive vehicle, the front wheels get moved to the back, but do not change sides. The rear wheels move forward and change sides. On a rear wheel drive, the back tires get moved to the front without changing sides. The front tires move to the back and change sides. On a four wheel or all wheel drive the front right and back left wheel change places, and the front left and back right change places.

In some cases you may have unidirectional tires. To rotate these correctly, switch the right back and with the right front and the left back with the left front.

Changing Tires

Removing the tire is the first step in getting your vehicle back on the road when you are faced with a flat. If possible position your car on a level surface. If this is not possible, put a large rock on the downhill side of the diagonally opposite wheel to prevent the car form rolling. You will need lug nut wrench and a car jack. Take off the hubcap, if you need to. Use the wrench to loosen the lug nuts. Use the car jack to raise up your car. See your operator's manual for the safest jack position. Raise the car high enough to remove the tire. Remove the lug nuts all the way. Pull of the tire and set it aside.

Having just removed a flat, your car will be up on a jack and ready to receive the new tire. Lift the new or spare tire up onto the wheel. Make sure the air valve faces outward. Replace each lug nut. Do not tighten them down immediately. Once they are all on, tighten the top lug nut part way, then tighten the opposite lug nut part way. Do the one to the right or left of the top next, and then its opposite. Continue moving around the wheel in this pattern until you have tightened all the lug nuts. Carefully lower the jack. Tighten each lug nut one more time. Make sure they are as tight as possible. Replace the hubcap.

Changing a tire is a common task, and you should keep the tools in your vehicle to make a tire change possible. Make sure you have a lug nut wrench or tire iron, a car jack, a spare tire, and a canister of penetrating oil. The oil can be used to help loosen a stuck lug nut. Check the pressure on your spare tire each month—you don't want to be faced with a flat and find out your spare is flat, too.

When you go to remove a tire from the wheel studs, use care. If the tire is worn, there may be protruding steel that can cut your hands. Remember that a car can slip off its jack. Never get under a car being held up by a tire-changing jack.

Motor Oil

Motor Oil Weight

Motor oil helps your engine to run smoothly. It keeps all the moving parts within an engine lubricated and it prevents them from fusing when an engine becomes hot. Viscosity is what allows motor oil to do this. The term viscosity refers to the thickness of a liquid. The numbers, or weights, listed on a motor oil container refer to its viscosity. A low number means the oil is thinner or has lower viscosity. A higher number means a thicker oil. Viscosity changes with temperature. At higher temperatures liquids lose viscosity. To counteract viscosity loss as engine heat rises, many motor oils have a dual-weight. This means they have one viscosity at a low temperature and a different viscosity at a high temperature. To create this effect, polymers are added to the oil. As the oil heats, the polymers unwind preventing it from losing viscosity. Refer to your vehicle's operator's manual to find the oil weight you should use.

Checking Oil

As a general rule of thumb, you should have your car's oil changed every 3 months or every 3000 miles. That means if you drive less than 3000 miles in 3 months, you can change it less often. If you drive more than 3000 miles in 3 months, you should change it every 3 months.

At times, you may need to check your oil. You'll need a rag to do so. Open your car's hood. Locate the lid of the oil chamber. It will usually have a picture of an oilcan on it. Most vehicles have a dipstick attached to the lid. Unscrew the lid and carefully remove the dipstick. Clean the end of the stick and reinsert it into the chamber. Pull it out again and look at how far along the stick the oil has reached. The dipstick has markings on it, so you can tell if there is enough oil in the chamber.

Changing the Oil

An oil change is routine maintenance that most car owners now choose to leave to a professional. It is, however, a straightforward procedure that a car owner can do. You will need a way to safely elevate your car, old rags, an oil pan, and a socket wrench. First elevate the vehicle so that you can slide under it. Find the oil plug, and place the oil pan under it. Use the socket wrench to loosen the oil plug. Then remove it by hand. The oil will rush out, and it may be hot, so use care. Allow the oil to drain completely. Wipe down the plug and replace. Next locate the oil filter. Place the oil pan under the filter. Unscrew the oil filter and remove it. Allow any remaining oil to drain. Rub a small amount of oil on the rubber seal and then install the new rubber filter. Don't forget to add oil to the engine when you are finished!

Checking Radiator Fluid

In newer model cars, there is an engine coolant reservoir that you can check even when the car is still hot. To check your engine coolant, release and open the hood. Locate the radiator. It will be at the front of the engine, usually right behind the hood release. Find the plastic reservoir tank. It will have a tube leading from it to the radiator. Unscrew the lid and look inside to determine coolant levels. Add coolant if necessary.

In older vehicles, you will have to check the fluid levels inside the radiator. It is only safe to do this when a car is cool. Opening the radiator of a hot car can lead to burns. The fluid should fill the radiator. If not, add coolant.

If you find your car requires you to add coolant often, have it checked by a mechanic. There may be a leak.

Checking Vehicle's Belts

A vehicle uses a number of belts to work properly. There is a timing belt in the engine. Power steering, the alternator, the air condition, and the fan may also use a belt. If you check the state of the belts every few months, you can determine if they need to be replaced before they break or wear out completely. This can save labor costs, and a planned repair is easier to manage than an emergency repair.

To check your belts, choose a time when your car is cool. Open the hood. Locate each belt. Use your thumb and press lightly against each one. You should not be able to move it more than an inch in either direction. If you can or if the belt appears cracked, then it needs to be replaced.

Windshield Wiper Fluid

Keeping your windshield wiper fluid full is important. Part of safe driving is maintaining good visibility through the windshield. The windshield wiper fluid is a tool that helps you do this.

To check and refill your wiper fluid, open the hood of your car. Look for a plastic reservoir with blue fluid in it. There should be a tube going from it in the direction of the windshield. Unscrew the cap and pour in more fluid if necessary.

The windshield wiper fluid reservoir may look very similar to the engine coolant reservoir. Make sure you are adding wiper fluid to the correct reservoir. If you aren't certain, check your operator's manual before adding any fluid.

Always use windshield wiper fluid rather than water. It contains detergents that help clean your windshield better. It also has antifreeze in it to keep it from freezing in cold weather.

Keeping Windshield Fog-Free

Because visibility is important to safe driving, you must keep your windshield from fogging up. Modern cars have a defrost setting as part of the heating and air conditioning system. Running the heater on this setting will help to clear the windshield.

Car windows are more prone to build up than building or home windows. The plastics in the car release vapors. In the contained space, those vapors can lead to a film on the windows. Take the time every other week to wash the inside windows of your car.

Car windows are more likely to fog over when humidity is high. Do what you can to reduce the moisture in your car. Shake off wet items like jackets and umbrellas before getting into the car and crack the front windows to reduce humidity. If your vehicle's windows are fogged up, allow them time to clear before you start driving.

Batteries

Your car's battery is what makes it possible to start the car. If the battery runs down, your car won't start. Periodically you should check the battery and make sure it is in good working order. Open the hood and locate the battery. Check the battery's connector cables. They should not move at all. If they are loose, tighten them down. Check that the battery is secure within the battery tray. Again if it is loose, tighten it. Check the water level within the battery. Open the plastic cover and look inside. Water should be visible. If not, add distilled water. Finally, check the battery terminals where the cables connect. If they have a crusty build up, it's time to clean them. Use wire brush and baking soda mixed with water. If you have an older battery, it may be time to replacc, especially if winter is coming and you live in a cold climate. A general guideline is to replace your battery every four years.

Replacing an old battery with a new one is a straightforward procedure, and a process you can do yourself if you'd rather not pay a mechanic. To replace a battery, you must first remove the old one. First detach the black cable. Loosen it with a wrench, and then remove it with your hands. Next, detach the red cable. If either cable sticks, you can use a screwdriver to pry them loose. Next use a wrench to remove the clamp that holds the battery in place. Remove the battery from the tray. Use care—it's heavy. Clean the battery tray and connector cables. Now place the new battery in the tray. Affix the clamp that will hold it in place. Make sure it is tight. Then attach the red cable followed by the black cable. Make sure you match the cables up to their proper terminals.

Winterizing a Vehicle

Winter weather can be rough on a car. It also presents additional driving hazards not seen in other seasons. Take some time in late fall to prepare your car for winter. Begin by taking car of any scheduled maintenance. Whether your car is due for an oil change or a full service tune up, the time leading into winter is the perfect time to do it. Replace the windshield wiper blades. They have to work harder in the winter, so a fresh pair is a good plan. Drain your engine coolant and replenish it with new coolant. Top off your windshield wiper fluid. Check that your battery is clean and tightly connected. If it is more than four years old, have it replaced before winter. Check that your tires are in good repair and have proper pressure. Check the spare, too. Finally, put a road kit in your trunk that includes blankets, flares, extra gloves, kitty litter for traction, and an ice scraper and compact snow shovel.

Replacing Headlights

Sooner or later a headlight bulb on your car will go out and require replacement. In most cases, this is a simple procedure. Determine whether the specific bulb you need to replace is a high-beam bulb or a low-beam bulb. You'll need to know the make, model, and year of your car to ensure you get the correct size and style bulb. Once you've purchased the replacement bulb, you're ready to change your car's headlight. Open the hood, and locate the backside of the headlight. Find the retaining ring, and unscrew it. Pull backward to remove the socket and bulb. Disconnect the old bulb, and plug in the new bulb. Test that the new headlight works before replacing the bulb and socket. Once you've put the bulb and socket back, screw down the retaining ring.

While replacement bulb headlights have become more common, many older vehicles use sealed-beam headlights. These headlights are bigger and have the silver reflective surface built in. Determine which size sealed beam headlight you need. Once you have the replacement headlight, you are ready to make the switch. You have to remove sealed beam headlights from the front rather than from the back. In some cases this means you will have to remove some trim pieces. Use care in doing so, and pay attention to how these pieces will fit back onto the car. Once you've exposed the sealed beam headlights, locate and unscrew the retaining screws. Pull the unit gently toward you. Detach it from the socket, and then attach the new headlight. Push it back into place, reaffix the retaining screws, and then reattach any trim pieces you had to remove.

DETERMINING HEADLIGHT ALIGNMENT

Headlight alignment is important because it determines whether or not your lights are illuminating the road directly in front of you. Misaligned lights can also cause discomfort to oncoming drivers. To determine if your lights are aligned, find a wall, garage door, or other flat, vertical surface that you can park 25 feet away from with your headlights facing the surface. When it is dark outside, turn your headlights on and look at where they hit the surface. Properly aligned headlights will hit the surface directly in front of you. Both lights will create a light spot that is parallel to the ground. If your lights are not properly aligned you can adjust the two aiming screws located by each light, or take it to a professional to have the lights aligned.

YEARLY MAINTENANCE

By getting regularly scheduled maintenance performed on your vehicle you can keep your fuel efficiency high and reduce the number of breakdowns and costly repairs you experience.

The first component of a yearly maintenance plan is regular self-administered maintenance. Check the cars fluid levels, headlights and signals, and belts each month. Make sure fluids are topped off, all lights are functioning and clean, and that the belts are in good repair. Also check the tire pressure each month.

Next, depending on how many miles you drive, plan to have your car's oil changed three or four times each year. Usually, the mechanic will also check fluid levels and the condition of your air filter at this time.

Finally, schedule a yearly tune up for your car. The mechanic should check your spark plugs and fuel injector, cleaning or replacing them if necessary. A tune up may also involve a check of your car's suspension, alignment, and cooling system.

TRANSMISSION

The transmission in your vehicle is responsible for changing the speed ratio between the motor and the wheels. The engine in a car has a fairly small range of speeds, but varying driving conditions require that a wide range of speeds and power be available. The transmission allows you to take advantage of different gear ratios. This means you can have differing levels of power and differing top speeds in each gear. This allows you to accelerate smoothly from a stop, drive up a hill, and cruise at freeway speeds all with equal ease. Without a transmission, your vehicle would be limited to a single gear ratio. If it were the equivalent of first gear, you would be able to accelerate and drive up hills, but you wouldn't be able to drive at high speeds. If you had only third gear, acceleration would be difficult and slow. Driving at speeds between 30 and 45 miles per hour would be comfortable. Freeway speeds would be possible but would tax the engine.

ANTI-LOCK BRAKES

Anti-lock brakes are an important safety feature that many cars have. The stopping ability of your vehicle is affected by a number of factors. The condition of your tires and the condition of the road are the two most important. Coming to a fast and complete stop when the road is slippery is very difficult with standard brakes, even if your tires are good condition. The brakes will typically lock up, your tires will lose their grip on the road, and you will go into a skid. Anti-lock brakes are equipped with a speed sensor that detects when your tires are about to lock up. Anti-lock brakes use a valve, a pump, and a computer controller to vary the pressure from the brakes to the tires to keep the tires from locking up.

Catalytic converters

All cars produce pollution. In the interest of reducing pollution output, and to comply with local, state, and federal, emissions laws, car manufacturers equip cars with a catalytic converter. The catalytic converter uses materials like platinum and rhodium to attract certain molecules, preventing them from entering the atmosphere as pollutants. Most catalytic converters have two sections that neutralize pollutants. The first is the reduction chamber. It reduces nitrous oxide emissions by bonding the nitrogen molecules and allowing the oxygen molecules to pass through. The second is the oxidation chamber. Through a similar process is reduces the emission of unburned hydrocarbons and carbon monoxide. A third part of the catalytic converter monitors the oxygen in the emissions and adjusts the fuel injection system to keep the engine running smoothly and as cleanly as possible.

Carburetors

Older model cars used a carburetor to move fuel into the engine. For an engine to fire properly, it requires the proper mix of fuel and air. The carburetor's job was to provide the engine the proper mix. To little air would prevent the engine from running or potentially damage the engine. Too much air would flood the engine or waste fuel. As engines became more complicated, more was demanded from carburetors. Different circuits were added to mix fuel properly for different situations: cruising, idling, accelerating, towing, and cold weather starts. Because of the growing complications of producing a carburetor that could meet all an engines different needs and because of increasing stringency regarding emission controls, carburetors were phased out in favor of fuel injection systems.

Fuel injection systems

When carburetors became impractical, they were replaced by fuel injection systems. A modern fuel-injection system is a multi-port system—it has a fuel injector for each engine cylinder. This design allows the fuel injector to provide the precise fuel-to-air ratio needed and to react quickly to changing driving situations. The air that enters the engine is controlled in part by pressure you put on the gas pedal. The gas pedal is connected to a throttle valve. More pressure on the gas pedal releases more air into the engine. The engine's computer responds by releasing more fuel into the engine. The engine computer controls the fuel injectors, triggering the proper one to stay open for the proper amount of time. Each fuel injector atomizes the fuel into a mist when it releases it into the engine making it easier to burn.

Mufflers

A car produces more than one kind of pollution when it runs. Not only does the engine produce chemical byproducts that need to be minimized, it also produces noise. The car's muffler works to reduce he level of the engine's noise, helping to control noise pollution. A muffler is actually a set of tubes with precisely placed holes drilled into them. The tubes reflect the engine's sound in such a way that it is canceled out. Your ear hears the sum of the sounds around you. By reflecting your engine's sound in a way that creates an opposite sound wave, the muffler actually cancels out a large portion of the engine's noise.

Flushing the engine

Many auto dealers and oil change facilities offer an engine flush service. This service forces fluid through the engine in the opposite direction that the fluid normally travels. It releases carbon deposits and is supposed to quickly clean the engine. An engine flush can have negative consequences. The carbon deposits that it breaks free can actually clog your fuel filter and reduce performance. In the interest of preventative maintenance, it is best to change your engine oil every three months or 3000 miles. This will keep the engine clean and negate the need for an engine flush. Even a neglected engine can be better cleaned over time by regular maintenance than by an engine flush.

Engine Cooling System

An engine's job is to convert fuel into mechanical energy. It's an inefficient process. About 70% of the potential energy is lost as heat. This tremendous amount of heat must be addressed or the engine will be damaged. The cooling system's primary job is to keep the engine from overheating. An engine runs most efficiently when the coolant maintains a constant temperature of 200 degrees Fahrenheit, so the coolants secondary job is to maintain a constant temperature within the engine. Most cars have a liquid cooling system to perform these two functions. Liquid coolant moves from the reservoir into pipes that pass through the engine. The coolant absorbs heat from the engine. When the coolant passes through the radiator it releases the heat into the air. This achieves both goals, preventing overheating and keeping the engine temperature constant.

Transmission

Adaptive Automatic Transmission

An automatic transmission changes gears for you to adapt speed and power needs as you drive. An adaptive automatic transmission can learn your driving style and adjust shift points and other functions to suit your individual needs and to improve efficiency.

Continuously Variable Transmission

Most transmissions use gears to adjust the power output from the engines to the wheels. A continuously variable transmission doesn't have any gears. It works very much like an automatic transmission, but power is transferred and adjusted continuously from the engine to the wheels.

Airbags

Curtain Side Airbags

These kinds of airbags deploy from above the side windows, both in the front and back. They engage in the event of a collision from the side or if sensors detect that the car is about to roll over. Curtain side airbags protect the heads of both the passengers and the driver. They also help to protect from broken glass.

Dual Front Airbags

These air bags are located in the steering wheel and in the passenger-side dashboard. These airbags are designed to protect both the front-seat passenger and the driver from a collision from the front. Most front airbags use sensors to determine how quickly they need to deploy. They will come out more gently in a minor collision, which can help reduce airbag-related injuries.

Dual-Stage Airbags

These airbags have two levels or deployment. How they deploy is determined by how much force there is in the collision.

Break Downs

If your vehicle breaks down on the highway, it is imperative you alert other drivers to the hazard of your stalled vehicle. First turn on your hazard lights. These blinking yellow lights alert other drivers that there is a problem. If it is dark outside, leave your headlights on. If you have them available, place roadside flares approximately 200 feet behind your stalled vehicle to give approaching drivers ample warning of a problem. If you do not have flares, find a safe place you can stand about

200 feet back from your vehicle and wave the approaching cars around. Remain a safe distance from traffic when doing this.

Bicycles

Bicyclists are more vulnerable than passengers in vehicles. Therefore you, as a driver, need to take extra care when driving around bicycles. The rules to sharing the road with bicyclists are as follows:

1. When bicycles are in a marked or unmarked crosswalk, they have the right-of-way. You must stop for them.
2. If you are crossing a sidewalk to enter a driveway or parking lot, yield to bicyclists using the sidewalk.
3. Do not drive or park in bicycle lanes. (You may cross them to make turns or enter traffic.). Yield to bicyclists using the lanes.
4. Always pass bicyclists with extra caution. Be certain you allow enough room that there is no chance your vehicle will come into contact with them.

Bicyclists have responsibilities when riding on roads, too. They must keep as far to the right of the road as they safely can. They may move left into traffic if they intend to turn left or if they are passing another bicyclist. Bicyclists must yield to pedestrians in crosswalks or on sidewalks. When riding on a road or using a bike lane, multiple bicyclists should travel either single file or two-by-two. Bicyclists must use hand signals when turning. They must wear reflectors at night. They must keep at least one hand on their handlebars at all times. Bicycles must have brakes that are in good working order. They must not carry passengers unless the bike is built with more than one seat.

Avoiding Collisions

If a collision seems imminent, you can often avoid it or reduce the damage by stopping, turning, or speeding up. You as the driver must decide the best action.

- When stopping, if your vehicle has antilock brakes, press firmly on the brake pedal until you come to a stop. Without antilock brakes depress the brake as firmly as possible without causing the brakes to lock. If you begin to skid, let up on the brake until you regain control, then press it down again.
- If a sudden turn is required and you have antilock brakes, you can brake and turn at the same time. Otherwise, apply the brakes briefly to slow down, then turn. If you have the choice of running off the road or being in a head-on collision, running off the road is usually the safer option.
- If a vehicle is going to hit you from behind or from the side, speeding up may be your best choice.
- If you are involved in a collision, do what you can to reduce your injuries and to prevent a secondary collision.
- If a vehicle hits you from behind, press yourself backwards into your seat and press your head against the headrest. If needed, press the brakes to stop your vehicle from hitting the next car in front of you.
- If you are hit from the side, you may to steer the vehicle use the brakes to avoid a secondary collision.
- If you are hit from the front, try to turn your vehicle before the collision so that you receive only a glancing blow. This will reduce the damage and risk of injuries. Your air bag may deploy, so be prepared.
- Always use a seatbelt with a shoulder restraint. It will reduce injuries should a collision occur.

Skidding

When a vehicle's tires lose their grip on the road, the vehicle goes into a skid. Skids generally happen when you are going faster that you should be given current road conditions, and it is safest to avoid a skid in the first place. If you do go into a skid, don't panic. Many drivers impulsively use the brake, which can make the skid worse. Instead of braking, you should focus on steering. Turn your steering wheel in the direction you want the car to go. Once it moves that way, turn the steering wheel in the opposite direction. Repeat this process of corrective steering until you regain control of the vehicle.

Approaching a Collision

When you approach a collision that you were not involved in and did not witness, keep your eyes on the road, stay alert for distracted drivers that may be around, and move with the flow of traffic until you have passed. Do not stop at the scene of an accident unless emergency help has not yet arrived and you are qualified to render assistance. (Assistance may be as simple as calling emergency response on your cell phone, so consider all the ways you may be of help if help has not yet arrive.).

If emergency vehicles are on the scene, stay alert for emergency personnel. Follow any instructions they may give you. Take care to stay out of their way.

Parked Car Collision

If you should happen to hit a park car that damages the vehicle in question, you have an obligation to stop and attempt to locate the damaged car's owner. If the car is parked in front of a house, knock at the house to see if the owner is present. If it is parked at a single business, check inside to see if you can find the owner. If the car is parked at a mall or on a street with many places the owner might be, wait as long as possible to see if you can speak with the owner. If you cannot locate the owner and cannot wait for his or her return, leave a note somewhere on the damaged vehicle with your contact information and insurance information. Also include the date and time of the accident.

Collision without Injuries

If you are in a collision with another vehicle, you need to stop, but you must do so safely. Move your vehicle out of the flow of traffic. Use your emergency flashers to warn other vehicles. If flares are available, set them out as a warning. If your vehicle is extremely damaged or if it is smoking, turn off the ignition. Maintain awareness of the traffic patterns around you to avoid being struck by another vehicle. Once you have reduced or eliminated any ongoing hazard from your wrecked vehicle, exchange contact and insurance information with the other driver involved in the collision. It is your responsibility to have your vehicle moved to a safe location as soon as possible. Do not leave it on the shoulder or meridian of a roadway. If it is not drivable, contact someone to have it towed.

Collision with Injuries

If you are involved in a collision and someone on the scene is injured, your first responsibility is to call for help. Use a cell phone to call 911. If you do not have a cell phone, flag someone down and request to use their cell phone or ask them to go make the call. Do not move an injured person unless they are in immediate danger from an explosion or from surrounding traffic. If more than one person is injured, check the people who are not able to walk or talk first. Assess their injuries. If someone is bleeding, apply pressure to the wound. If someone seems in danger of going into shock, cover him with a blanket to keep him warm.

PEDESTRIANS

Because of their vulnerability, pedestrians always merit extra attention and caution, but in three situations, you must remain very alert around pedestrians. When pedestrians walk in the street because there is no sidewalk (or instead of a provided sidewalk), give them as much space as you safely can. Remain ready for unpredictable movements. Pedestrians should walk on the left side of the road, facing traffic. Pay special attention to pedestrians walking with their backs toward you. They do not see you coming and they may not hear your approach. Always be on the alert for pedestrians walking at night. People walking at night should wear white or reflective clothing, but they do not always do so. A pedestrian may be difficult to see at night.

A PEDESTRIAN'S RESPONSIBILITIES

There are a number of things that a pedestrian can do to increase safety levels when walking in the vicinity of traffic. First, pedestrians should walk on the left side of the street. By walking toward oncoming traffic, you ensure that you will see cars as they approach. You can also signal to a car with your arms if you believe that a driver has not seen you and may hit you. Pedestrians should use sidewalks whenever they are available and should cross streets at marked crosswalks whenever possible. If not crosswalk is available, cross at corners rather than in the middle of blocks. If a sidewalk is not available, stay as far off the road as possible. Finally, at night pedestrians should wear white or reflective clothing to be better seen by drivers.

MOTORCYCLES

Motorcycle riders are more vulnerable to injury than passengers in a car should an accident occur. A driver needs to take extra caution around motorcycles because of this. There are a number of things you should consider regarding motorcycles. First they are small and fast. They can seem to appear alongside of your vehicle when they weren't there a moment before. Always take note of motorcycles you see in your rearview mirror, so they don't surprise you if they overtake you. Because they are small, motorcycles may be hidden behind vehicles or on the other side of vehicles, making you unaware of them. They are also easier to lose in your blind spot. For these two reasons always check your mirror and your blind spot before changing lanes.

RESPONSIBILITIES OF MOTORCYCLISTS

A motorcycle driver has extra vulnerabilities when driving and therefore has extra responsibilities to ensure his or her safety and the safety of passengers. A motorcycle is capable of driving much faster than most vehicles. However, a motorcyclist is still legally bound to travel at or below posted speed limits. A motorcyclist must be aware that they are less visible than other vehicles on the road. If you are driving a motorcycle, be prepared for vehicles to cut you off and don't travel in a vehicle's blind spot. As a motorcycle driver, it is important you choose proper attire. Long pants and a jacket, both made or a tough material, give good coverage and can help to reduce injuries should you be involved in an accident. Also, whether it is the law or not, use a full-face helmet that is thick enough to protect your head from injury. Require the same of any passengers.

The most common situation in which an automobile and motorcycle collide is during a left hand turn. When a car is making a left hand turn across an intersection and a motorcycle is approaching from the opposite direction, it is difficult for the driver of the car to accurately judge the motorcycle's speed of approach. This is because motorcycles are smaller than cars—their smaller profile makes it appear as if they are going slower than they are. A car that misjudges a motorcycle's speed may proceed to make a left hand turn. If the motorcycle is too close, this will result in a collision. The best thing for automobile drivers making left turns to do is yield to approaching motorcycles.

Semi-Trucks

A distracted driver or one who is not alert or informed can create a number of hazards driving around large semi-trucks. First, these trucks have several large blind spots. Do not drive directly behind a semi-truck unless you are following at a distance and can see the driver's side mirrors. Do not cruise at the side of a semi-truck for any length of time. The driver may not see you and may attempt to change lanes. When driving around semi-trucks, remember that they stop much more slowly than the average car. Avoid coming to a sudden stop in front of one. Also, give semis more room when going down a hill. It is easy for them to gain speed on a downgrade. They will travel more slowly going up hills, so do not follow them closely as you approach a hill.

Responding to Emergency Vehicles

When you hear an emergency vehicle's siren or see its lights flashing, immediately slow down. Use your signal and begin to pull as far to the right side of the road as you can so the emergency vehicle may pass you. Come to a stop until the emergency vehicle has passed, then carefully, using your signal, return to your lane. If you cannot see the vehicle, but hear its siren, slow down and prepare to pull over. Do not pass through any intersections until you have located the emergency vehicle. Doing so could cause a collision with the emergency vehicle. If a police officer pulls behind you and flashes his lights or turns on his siren, immediately pull over to the side of the road and wait for the officer to approach your vehicle.

Highway Hypnosis and Velocitation

Highway Hypnosis is a condition that occurs when long drives require ongoing concentration. It's characterized by the driver feeling dull or droopy-eyed and "zoning out" while focused on the passing road. It can result in slower reaction times or in a driver not noticing a potential hazard soon enough to avoid it. The best way to prevent this from happening is to take frequent breaks to stretch and take your mind and eyes off the road.

Velocitation is the misperception of speed that occurs when you move from traveling on a fast road to traveling on a slow road. It becomes easy to inadvertently speed and puts you in danger of a receiving a speeding ticket.

Required Extra Space

In some situations, it is prudent to give vehicles or pedestrians more space than you normally would.

- Give any driver or pedestrian with compromised visibility extra space--Drivers who are backing out of roadways, pedestrians carrying packages or umbrellas that obstruct their view, and pedestrians with their backs to you are all examples.
- Watch for people who are distracted--Children, drivers who are multitasking (talking on a cell phone or reading a map), and construction workers are all examples of people who may not be aware you are there.
- Look for signs of confusion--A confused driver or a driver who shows signs of being indecisive needs extra space. They may make unpredictable decisions. Allow yourself extra room to react to unexpected movements.
- Give room to drivers making poor decisions--When a driver passes you inappropriately or tries to move into your lane even though there is not enough room, give him extra space to safely complete his action.

PURCHASING A CAR

When a person, especially a young person, decides to purchase a car, there are a number of factors to consider. The most obvious is financial. Before buying a car, you must analyze what you can afford. If you plan to finance a car, you must consider the monthly payment and the long-term cost of interest on a loan. You must consider the consequences if you are unable to make payments. You must also think about driving and maintenance costs. When you purchase a car, in addition to the monthly payment, there are gas expenses, insurance costs, and maintenance and repair costs. Besides the costs of a car, a young person should be encouraged to consider the reasons they wish to purchase a vehicle, what kind of driving they will be doing, how often they need a vehicle, and if their transportations needs wouldn't be better served through public means.

BUYING A USED CAR

A used car is often a smart buying decision, but in some ways it carries more risk than buying a new car. You can reduce your risk by making your buying decision carefully. Review car values and reliability reports online to make sure you are paying a fair price for a car that has a good record of reliability. Before buying a car, examine it thoroughly. Check the exterior for signs of damage. A car that has been in a collision or rollover is not a good car to buy. Check the interior. It should be clean and well maintained. Take the car for a test drive. Pay attention to any potential problems—odd noises that indicates a repair may be needed, panel warning lights that stay on, an unusual pull to one side or the other. If possible, have the vehicle undergo a professional inspection. (You'll have to pay for this service, so only take this step if you plan to buy.) Finally, make all financial arrangements in writing.

INSURANCE RATES

Insurance companies determine a driver's premium rates based on their assessment of a driver's risk level. A high-risk driver is more likely to be in a collision and therefore costs more to insure. Insurance companies look at a number of factors to determine a driver's risk. They look at gender. They consider age—younger drivers are inexperienced and considered a higher risk. They will look at how many miles you drive each week. More time on the road raises risk. They consider marital status—married couples are considered safer drivers than single people. They also consider the type of car you are buying insurance for, your driving record (any previous accidents or citations), and where you live. Many insurance companies also consider a car's safety features, and if you are a student, your grade point average.

MANDATORY INSURANCE

Car accidents are common. Rather than tie up small municipal courts determining who is at fault for an accident and what compensation the guilty party owes the other party, insurance is mandated by law. Insurance companies determine fault in an accident. The insurance provider of the driver at fault pays the victim for damages.

Carrying insurance is financially responsible. It means if you are in a collision and found to be at fault, you will not have to bear the financial burden of paying for damages. You will pay a small deductible and your insurance company will pay the remaining costs. To provide this financial security, insurance companies charge a price. This is referred to as the premium.

INSURANCE TYPES

LIABILITY INSURANCE

This kind of insurance protects the people other than you involved in an accident with your vehicle. There are two types of liability insurance that most states require you to carry. Bodily injury insurance pays injury and death claims that result from your car injuring someone and legal costs associated with those claims. Property damage insurance pays for damage your car does to property.

Collision Insurance

This kind of insurance will pay you up to the listed value of your car if it is damaged in an accident, even if you are at fault. You must pay a deductible. The insurance covers everything beyond the deductible. States do not require collision insurance but if you drive a vehicle you have financed, most lenders require it.

Comprehensive Insurance

This kind of insurance covers damage to your vehicle not covered by collisions. Vandalism and fire are examples. Comprehensive insurance carries a deductible.

Insurance Amount

The state you live in will require you to carry a minimum level of bodily injury, total accident and property damage liability insurance. Think carefully about how much insurance you purchase. Often the state's minimum requirements are lower than what you can expect to owe if you get into an accident. A common recommendation, if you can afford it, is to purchase $100,000 per person for bodily injury, $300,000 per accident, and $50,000 in property damage. Having enough insurance is particularly important if you have assets (a house, for example) to protect. If the damage done in an accident exceeds your coverage, legal proceedings can jeopardize your assets.

Needed Information After Accident

If you are in an accident, there is quite a bit of information that you should collect from other drivers involved and from people who witnessed the accident. It's important to remain calm, so that you don't overlook this important step. You will need the names, driver license numbers, addresses, and phone numbers of all drivers involved. You will also need the names of their insurance companies and their policy numbers. It's a good idea to record the make, color, model, year, and license plate number of all vehicles involved. If someone other than the owner is driving any of the vehicles, also collect the name and phone number of the owner. Get contact information for any passengers and witnesses. If a police officer responds to the scene, record his name and badge number. Finally, write down the location of the accident, too. Having all this information will help process your insurance claim, and assist with any legal proceedings that may result from the accident.

If you are involved in an accident, there are a number of questions your insurance company will ask you. It's best if you write down the details of the accident while it is still fresh in your mind. After you've collected the contact information of everyone involved and from witnesses, write down the details surrounding the events of the accident. Include what had happened leading up to the accident, if any vehicles were not functioning properly before the accident (a broken headlight, for example), and if you noticed any pre-existing damage to a vehicle before the accident. Also write down the weather, time of day, and road conditions. Write down any special circumstances. If any of the drivers appear under the influence of drugs or alcohol, take note. If any of the drivers were talking on a cell phone at the time of the collision, write that down. If anything is unusual or if a driver makes a comment about the accident's cause, you should make a record of it.

School Buses

When approaching a school bus with its stop sign extended or with its flashing red lights turned on, you must stop. If you are traveling the same direction as the school bus, stop behind the bus. If you are traveling in the opposite direction of the bus, stop before you reach the bus. In some situations, you do not have to stop if you are traveling in the opposite direction of the school bus: if there are more than three marked lanes of traffic, if there is a median dividing the highway, or if there is a physical barrier separating the two directions of traffic.

If you are required to stop for a school bus, do not begin to move again until the stop sign has been retracted and/or the red flashing lights have been turned off. When it is okay to begin moving again, use caution and be mindful of children.

ORGAN DONOR STATUS

Organ donor status means that you have decided in the event of your death to donate any viable organs to those who may need them. Organ transplantation is a proven medical procedure. It can make an important life-changing—and often life-saving—difference to the organ recipient. The tissues and organs from a single donor can benefit up to 200 people. Every year 12,000 people in need of organ transplants die. This is due in part to people not sharing their decision to be an organ donor with their loved ones. You can have your organ donor status listed on your driver's license. To make this decision alone, you must be at least 18 years old. If you are under 18, you must have a parent or guardian's consent.

WORK ZONES

A work zone is an area where construction or maintenance work is taking place. It will be designated by orange signs with black letter and will usually be marked off with large orange or orange and white cones. The signs will provide you with information on how to proceed. A work zone holds many potential distractions. There is often large equipment present. Some drivers may be curious about how the large machines work and may try to watch them and the road at the same time. There is a lot of activity in a work zone that can demand your attention. You need to remain mindful of the workers movements and any signals they give you. Also, there is the potential for loud, sudden sounds that can startle you or the drivers around you.

To pass safely through a work zone without endangering yourself or others, the first step is to maintain heightened awareness. Pay close attention the road in front of you and to the activity going on around you. Maintain a safe distance between yourself and the construction workers and equipment as well as between your vehicle and other cars. Also maintain a safe speed. Prepare yourself to respond quickly to changing situations. Adopt an attitude of patience. It can take extra time to move through a work zone, and you may spend have to spend a good deal of time stopped. By staying calm and remaining patient, you make yourself a safer driver in a work zone situation. Finally, follow all instructions given to you by signs and by workers on site.

In most states, you will suffer harsher penalties for breaking traffic laws while in a work zone. Speeding in a work zone usually carries a double-the-standard fine. Check your states laws to know exact details. Driving in a way that results in a collision in a work zone can also carry harsh penalties. If your decisions result in the injury of an on-site worker, you will be held responsible for those injuries and will have to pay medical expenses. If your decisions result in the death of someone in the work zone, in some states you could face vehicular manslaughter charges.

There are three things you should remember to help you drive safely in a work zone.

- First recognize the changing situation. Look for early warning signs that you are approaching a work zone. Often an orange sign with "work zone ahead" will be posted to warn drivers. Also watch for signs alerting you to closed lanes or changing traffic patterns. When in a work zone, recognize that there are extra hazards and remain aware.

- Second, react by responding appropriately to the work zone. Slow down to suggested speeds. Give other drivers and workers extra room. Follow directions.
- Third, remember that you are responsible for your driving decisions and can be held liable for mistakes you make while driving through a work zone, especially mistakes that endanger others.

Construction Workers Communication

There are four types of communication devices and methods that you can expect to find in and around work zones. They are signs, channelizing devices, lighting devices, and truck-mounted attenuators.

- Signs are generally orange with black writing. They are often reflective to make them readable at night. They give warnings of upcoming work zones and traffic pattern changes dues to work zones.
- Channelizing devices include cones and other devices that workers use to redirect traffic patterns around the work zone.
- Lighting devices are used much like signs to warn drivers of upcoming traffic pattern changes.
- Truck-mounted attenuators are used in particularly hazardous situations. The truck with a flashing amber light is parked 50 to 100 feet before the work zone to warn cars that they are approaching a work zone.

Determining Fault

Insurance companies and court systems typically determine which driver is at fault in the event of an accident. They take into account a number of factors including whether any drivers involved were under the influence of drugs or alcohol at the time, the road conditions, the traffic patterns, witness accounts, and police reports. If anyone has broken the law, the fault will be found with that driver. If the accident was a result of poor decisions by both or all drivers involved, insurance companies will assign fault in percentages to determine who is most at fault and how payouts will be made. If no independent witness are available and the drivers involved give conflicting accounts, insurance companies have to determine the more plausible circumstances in order to determine fault.

Stopped by Officer

If a police officer signals for you to pull over either by pulling in behind and flashing the police car lights or sounding the siren, pull over to the right hand side of the road in a safe fashion and come to a complete stop. Turn off the car. If it is nighttime, turn on the car's overhead light. Remain in your vehicle unless the officer requests you to exit. Keep your hands on your steering wheel as the officer approaches. Don't make any sudden movements, and don't attempt to reach into your wallet, purse, or glove compartment until the officer is at the window and has requested your registration, driver's license and proof of insurance. If you have a weapon in the vehicle, alert the officer that it is there and explain where it is located. Always follow the officer's instructions and don't argue with the officer.

Special License Types

States issue different types of driver licenses depending on the type of vehicle you plan to drive. Different licenses will often require you to pass additional knowledge-based and/or behind-the-wheel driver tests. The most common types of driver licenses include an operator's license for driving a standard passenger vehicle; a chauffeur's license for driving vehicles that transport people for payment including taxicabs and buses; a motorcycle endorsement for operating a motorcycle.

You would also need a special license or endorsement if you plan to drive a commercial vehicle, certain farming equipment or to transport hazardous waste.

IMPORTANT TERMS

Blind Hill: A blind hill is a hill that hides oncoming traffic. It is not safe to pass as you approach a blind hill. Also be prepared to react if an oncoming vehicle is attempting to pass.

Following Distance: This is the amount of distance you allow between yourself and the vehicle in front of you. On surface streets, you should follow at least two seconds behind the vehicle in front of you. On highways or freeways, increase your following distance to four seconds. Use a greater following distance when behind emergency vehicles, motorcycles, school buses, and semi-trucks.

Blind Spot: This is the area to either side of your vehicle that you cannot see with your mirrors. Always check your blind spot before changing lanes.

Helmet: A helmet is a safety device that should be worn by all motorcyclists, bicyclists and people operating motorized scooters. A full-face helmet that is thick enough to protect your skull provides the most protection.

Braking Distance: Your braking distance is how much distance it takes you to come to a complete stop. Braking distance will vary depending on the speed you are traveling and on the condition of the roads.

Conspicuous: This means easily seen. As a driver, you should strive to be conspicuous to those sharing the road with you.

Hand Signals: In the event that your vehicle's turn signals are malfunctioning, you can communicate your intent to turn or stop using hand signals.

Reaction Time: Your reaction time is how long it takes you to begin an action after you recognize that action is necessary. For example, it takes most drivers a half of a second to begin braking after they realize they need to brake.

Blind Curve: A blind curve is a curve in the road that prevents you from seeing oncoming traffic. Do not attempt to pass on a blind curve. Also be prepared for oncoming traffic that is passing unlawfully.

Cushion of Space: This refers to the area around your vehicle that you consciously attempt to leave clear so as to allow yourself somewhere to go should a collision become a potential threat.

Electronic Brake Force Distribution: This feature accompanies anti-lock braking systems in some vehicles. It uses sensors to equally distribute braking force between the front and back tires. This feature can improve brake performance and reduce the wear on brakes.

Hybrid Powertrain: One alternative to concerns regarding vehicle emissions is to purchase a hybrid vehicle. In a hybrid vehicle the car has both a gas-driven motor and an electric motor. It depends on the vehicle, which motor system dominates. These vehicles are becoming more readily available, and they can reduce fuel use and emissions.

Lane-Departure Warning System: A car equipped with a lane-departure warning system will sound an alarm when your vehicle crosses over the lane markers.

Oversteer: This refers to when a car's wheels lose traction and force the car in the direction of a turn. For example, turning to fast to the left may cause the car to spin to the left. It is most common in rear-wheel drive vehicles. To counteract oversteer, steer in the opposite direction and then correct. Use the brakes and gas pedal very gently.

Understeer: This refers to a car's wheels lose traction and resist moving in the direction of a turn. For example, when you try to steer into a turn, the vehicle's wheels lose traction and then the car continues straight. This usually happens in the snow or ice. It is most common in front-wheel drive vehicles. To counteract understeer, release the gas pedal, and gently brake.

Variable Valve Timing: In a vehicle equipped with variable valve timing, a computer alters the how the engine valves function to increase the engine's efficiency.

Traction Control: Some vehicles are equipped with a traction control system. When you accelerate, if the tires slip, the traction control system will automatically engage the brake just for a second to help the tires regain traction.

Rear-Obstacle Warning System: In a vehicle equipped with this system, an alarm will sound or a warning light will go off if a sensor on your rear bumper detects an object in the near proximity.

Navigation System: Many cars are equipped with an electronic navigation system that will display maps and generate directions.

Adaptive Cruise Control: Cruise control is a system that lets you maintain a constant speed without having to keep the accelerator pedal depressed. A standard cruise control system will maintain a constant speed regardless of forward obstacles. With and adaptive cruise control system, there are sensors on the front of the car that detect vehicles in front of you. The system will adjust your cruising speed to keep you a safe distant behind the next vehicle.

Air Suspension: Most suspension systems use springs to reduce a vehicles level of bounce in response to bumps in the road. Some cars use an air suspension system to provide a more comfortable ride.

Adjustable Suspension: Different spring tensions are more appropriate for different road conditions. An adjustable suspension system uses sensors to adjust spring tension to make it appropriate to your current road conditions.

Anti-Lock Brakes: An anti-lock brake system will automatically apply and release the brakes very quickly during stops on a slick surface or during panic stops. This keeps the tires from locking up and helps you maintain control of the vehicle.

Antiskid System: An antiskid system or an electronic stability system helps maintain traction during turning to prevent sideways skids. It works even if you do not use the brakes. Sensors detect when tires begin to lose traction and apply the brakes to the individual tires.

Automatic Transmission with Manual Shift Capability: Some cars come equipped with an automatic transmission that also has manual shift capability. When the car is in Drive the transmission functions automatically, but either a gearshift or buttons on the steering wheel allow the driver to determine when gear shifts are made, if desired.

Brake Assist: A feature that adds to your stopping power in emergency situations. Brake assist uses sensors to determine if brake assist is needed.

Traffic and Safety Regulations

VEHICLE REGISTRATION

Each state has its own laws when it comes to vehicle registration. Most states require you to register your vehicle in order to drive legally on public roads. When you register a vehicle, you will receive a license plate and a sticker with your registration's expiration date. You must renew your registration periodically. When you purchase a new vehicle, you must register it immediately. If you move from one state to another, you must register your vehicle in the new state within that state's required time period. In many densely populated areas, your vehicle must pass an emissions test before you can renew your registration. By requiring an emissions test, state's help improve air quality in problem areas.

VEHICLE TITLES

A vehicle's title is a legal document stating the vehicle's ownership. A title is usually required when you register your vehicle. In some cases, you may not have the original title for your vehicle. If you have lost your vehicle's title, you can contact the state that issued it originally and request a certified copy. If you are purchasing your vehicle on a loan, the loan issuer will often retain the title until you have paid for the vehicle in full. Again, if you need to show the title for any purpose, you can contact the loan issuer or the state and request a certified copy.

When you sell your vehicle, the title must be transferred to the new owner. At the time of the sale, both you and the purchaser must sign and date the title or certificate of ownership. The person purchasing the vehicle keeps the title. Depending on the laws of the state in which you reside, it is usually the responsibility of the purchaser to file for a transfer of ownership within a set period of time. As the seller, it is a good idea to file a transfer, too. If the new owner is involved in an accident before filing the transfer or forgets to file the paperwork, this action helps insulate you from liability. If you are purchasing a vehicle from a dealer, the responsibility of filing a transfer of ownership usually falls to the dealer. Check your state's laws.

LOSS OF LICENSE

There are more than a dozen reasons the state might choose to revoke your license. They include driving under the influence of a controlled substance, refusing to take a breathalyzer or blood test at the request of a police officer, being involved in a hit-and-run collision, providing fraudulent information to obtain a license, having no insurance and being involved in an accident, incurring too many traffic violations, using a vehicle to commit a felony, driving recklessly, failing to stop for a police vehicle that is trying to pull you over, not appearing in traffic court at a designated time, or driving with a license that has been suspended or that is fake.

INSURANCE REQUIREMENTS

In most states, drivers must carry liability insurance in order to drive. Auto insurance means that if you're involved in an accident that is determined to be your fault, your insurance company will pay for the damage that you've done beyond any deductible amounts. Insurance is important because property damage and injuries that result from accidents can cost thousands of dollars. Without insurance, you would be liable for these amounts, which could create a financial strain or result in court proceedings. Most states require all drivers to carry an insurance policy for both bodily injury and property damage. The amount of required coverage and the details of said coverage may vary from state to state. Check with the local department of motor vehicles to learn the requirements in your area.

TRAFFIC CONTROL

TRAFFIC CONTROL DEVICES

An all-encompassing term including all objects or personnel used to control the flow of traffic. Traffic control devices include traffic signs, traffic signals, pavement markings, and traffic-calming structures like roundabouts, slow speed bumps, or narrowed road sections.

TRAFFIC SIGNS

These include all posted signs designed to convey traffic rules, information about potential hazards, and directions. The information a sign is intended to convey can be quickly determined by its shape and color, even before the words or pictures on the sign are clear.

TRAFFIC SIGNALS

These are lights intended to tell you when to stop, proceed, or use caution. They include the standard red/yellow/green intersection lights, flashing red lights, and flashing yellow lights.

WHITE PAVEMENT LINES

A solid white pavement line is used to demark the right-hand edge of the road. On two lane highways, there is a white line on the outside edge of each lane as viewed with the flow of traffic. On a divided freeway or one lane road, there is a white line at the right of the right hand lane. You should stay to the left of solid white lines.

A dashed white line is used to separate lanes of traffic traveling in the same direction. You may change lanes when there is a dashed white line between you and the lane next to you. Sometimes you will find a solid white line between lanes of traffic traveling in the same direction. This indicates that it is hazardous to change lanes along that section of road. Unless an emergency or obstruction mandates it, you should wait until the line becomes dashed again before changing lanes.

YELLOW PAVEMENT LINES

A solid yellow pavement line will mark the left edge of the road on a one-way road.

On a two-lane highway, four possible yellow line combinations will separate you from oncoming traffic. The first is a single dashed yellow line. This indicates that you may pass slower vehicles in front of you provided the oncoming traffic lane provides enough clearance for you to do so safely. It also means that oncoming vehicles may pass from their lane as well. A dashed yellow line closest to you with a solid yellow line in the oncoming lane means you can pass if it is safe but the oncoming traffic is prohibited from passing. A solid yellow line that is closet to you accompanied by a dashed yellow line closer to the oncoming traffic means that oncoming vehicles may pass, but vehicles in your lane may not. A double yellow line dividing a two-lane highway means it is not safe to pass in either direction.

CROSSWALKS

Crosswalks at major intersections will have a traffic signal alerting pedestrians when they may safely cross. The crosswalk itself will usually be marked off with two wide white lines. For crosswalks that do not have a signal, they will be preceded by a warning sign (see below) and also usually marked off with two wide white lines.

When approaching a crosswalk without a signal, slow down and yield the right of way to any pedestrians waiting to cross. Whether the crosswalk has a signal or not, you must stop before the first wide white line. In some cases a crosswalk may not be marked with pavement lines. In those cases, you must still yield the right of way to waiting pedestrians or to people already in the crosswalk.

LEFT-HAND TURN LANE

Many roads will have a center lane for vehicles making left hand turns. A solid yellow line with an inner dashed yellow line will mark this lane. These markings are on both sides of the left-hand turn lane. This lane is reserved only for vehicles making a left-hand turn. Vehicles from either direction of traffic may use the left-hand turn lane. You may not use the left hand turn lane to pass. You may only travel 300 feet at the most in a left-hand turn lane before stopping to make your turn. Because the oncoming traffic may also use this lane, use caution when entering it—may sure you have a clear space to do so.

SIGNS

Warning Signs: These signs are generally yellow and often diamond shaped. They warn you of upcoming hazards or changes in the road.

Regulatory Signs: These signs are usually white or red. They convey instructions you have to follow, like "Stop" or "Do Not Pass" or the speed limit.

Work Area Signs: These signs convey information about road construction. They include flagger signs and detour signs. These signs are orange.

Service Signs: These signs tell where services like hospitals, pay phones, and gas stations are located. They are blue with white pictures or lettering.

Destination Signs: These signs convey exit information, distances to locations, and street names. They are green with white lettering.

These three signs are warning signs. They each alert you to an upcoming change in the road.

The first sign signifies that a previously divided highway is changing to an undivided highway. When you see this sign, you should plan to become more alert as you will be more exposed to oncoming traffic.

The second sign signifies that you will be moving from an undivided highway to a divided highway. You must pay attention for the upcoming median or divider.

The third sign signifies that you are approaching a steep or extended downgrade. Respond by being more alert to the trucks around you as they may lose their braking power and become a hazard.

These three signs are regulatory signs. They convey instructions that you must follow by law.

The first sign is a "Do Not Enter" sign. These signs are posted anywhere there is a risk of traffic entering a one-way street traveling the wrong way. You will see these signs posted at freeway exits warning drivers not to enter the freeway from that direction. As a driver, you create an immediate and extreme hazard if you disobey these signs.

The second sign conveys that you must turn left at an upcoming intersection.

The third sign conveys you must turn right at an upcoming intersection.

The second and third sign are often accompanied by arrows painted onto the lane, as well.

These are each warning signs that alert you to an upcoming change in the traffic pattern or in the road.

The first sign conveys a sharp curve the right. Slow down as you approach, so that your vehicle does not skid or spin out of control as you round the curve.

The second sign means traffic will be merging into the right hand lane from the right. If you are driving in the right hand lane, be alert for vehicles signaling to enter the flow of traffic. You may have to speed up or slow down, so that other vehicles can enter safely. If you are in the lane adjacent to the merge lane, be aware of drivers who need to change into your lane to make room for merging traffic.

These are each regulatory signs. You must obey the instructions they give.

The first sign is posted at a parking space that is reserved for disabled individuals. It is unlawful to park in a space with this sign unless you have a disabled parking permit.

The second sign is used when two lanes of traffic travel in the same direction, and the left lane is reserved for passing. When these signs are posted, remain in the right lane unless you are passing another slower vehicle. Do not cruise in the left lane.

The third sign prohibits a left-hand turn. Regulatory signs with a red circle and slash are prohibiting the action depicted.

Each of these signs is a warning signs regarding upcoming hazards or traffic changes.

The first sign denotes a school crosswalk. In most states, you must slow to 15 or 20 mph if children are present. If someone is waiting at the crosswalk, you must stop and allow them to cross.

The second sign tells you there is a railroad crossing ahead (sometimes, a railroad crossing sign is a white "X"). You must be alert for approaching trains. Remember to be certain you are able to proceed all the way across the train tracks before crossing them.

The third sign warns you that the right lane is ending. Traffic in the right lane needs to merge left. If you are in the right lane, signal, and look for a safe space to enter the left lane traffic. If you are in the left lane, be aware of vehicles merging into your lane and make space for them whenever you can safely do so.

These signs each warn you or potential hazards or upcoming traffic changes.

The first sign alerts you that a new lane is being added on the right side of the road. Traffic entering in this lane has its own lane. You should still be alert for anyone who is not paying attention and merges suddenly into your lane.

The second sign alerts you that there is a pedestrian crossing ahead—notice the shape is different than a school crossing sign. If anyone is waiting at the crosswalk, stop and allow them to cross.

The third sign alerts you that the road is slippery in wet conditions. If the roads are wet, decrease your speed accordingly.

These are each regulatory signs. You must follow the instructions given by these signs.

The first sign prohibits vehicles from turning right.

The second sign is used in multi-lane highways when more than one lane travels in the same direction. It instructs slow-moving vehicles, like large trucks or vehicles hauling trailers that they must stay in the right lane. Usually these signs are used where slower moving vehicles will have an even greater decrease in speed—on large hills, for instance.

The third sign is a speed limit sign. It designates the highest speed at which you may travel by law. Depending on road conditions, you may be required to drive more slowly than this speed, if safety mandates it.

These signs are regulatory signs giving mandatory instructions.

The first sign prohibits u-turns. Some states prohibit u-turns unless otherwise posted. Check your state laws to know which applies. If u-turns are generally prohibited, watch for u-turn permitted signs. If there isn't one, do not make a u-turn.

The second sign warns you that you are approaching a speed zone and will have to reduce your speed. Be ready to begin slowing down and be aware that other drivers will also be slowing down. Keep an eye on your rear view mirror as you are at higher risk of being rear-ended when braking is required.

The third sign notes that you may only travel straight ahead—turns are not permitted from the lane you are in.

The first sign is a railroad crossing warning. (In some cases, railroad-crossing signs are circular and yellow.) Stay on the alert for approaching trains and make sure the way is clear before you proceed over the railroad tracks.

The second sign is school speed zone sign. It means you must travel more slowly than the regularly enforced speed limit if there are children present. Most school speed limits are also enforced during certain hours of the day when more children are likely to be walking in the area.

The third sign is a "stop ahead" sign. It alerts you that you will need to stop at the upcoming intersection.

The first sign is a regulatory sign. It is a stop sign and it means you must come to a full, complete stop before proceeding through an intersection. Obey right-of-way rules to determine when it is your turn to go if more than one car comes to the intersection at the same time.

The second sign is a two-way highway sign. This means you will only be divided from oncoming traffic by lines drawn on the pavement. Drive defensively and stay alert.

The third sign alerts you that you may legally execute a u-turn at the intersection you are approaching. Always use extra caution when making a u-turn. Both drivers in oncoming lanes and those turning right into the lane you are turning into may not expect you to be there.

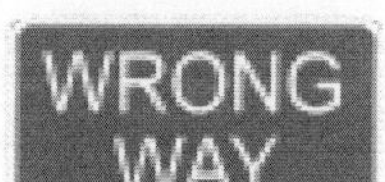

The first sign is a warning sign that alerts you to the fact that bicycles commonly share the road. Because cyclists are more vulnerable to injury than people traveling by car, use extra caution and courtesy around them.

The second sign is a regulatory sign that usually accompanies a "Do Not Enter" sign. It warns you that traffic in the posted lanes travels in the opposite direction and you should not turn into those lanes. Disobeying this sign creates an immediate hazard to yourself and those drivers around you.

The third sign alerts you to an approaching yield sign. Slow down your vehicle and be prepared to stop if necessary.

Learner's Permit vs License

A learner's permit is issued to an unlicensed driver who has passed a written knowledge exam regarding the rules of safe driving. A learner's permit allows the holder to drive when accompanied by a licensed adult. The learner permit makes it possible for an unlicensed driver to begin learning practical driving skills while supervised by a licensed driver.

A driver's license is issued when a driver has passed both a written knowledge exam and a behind-the-wheel drivers test.

Rules and regulations governing the issue of permits and licenses vary by state. Check with your local DMV to determine specific age restrictions and other restrictions.

Roadway Reflectors

Some roads have reflectors along the pavement lines. These reflectors help drivers to see where road markings are at night or in inclement weather. You may see three different colored reflectors on the road: white, yellow, or red.

- White reflectors are used along white pavement lines. They separate lanes traveling in the same direction. At night they will help you maintain a safe distance between your vehicle and vehicles in the next lane.
- Yellow reflectors are positioned along yellow pavement lines. They indicate the division from oncoming traffic.
- Red reflectors are used to indicate that you are traveling in the wrong direction for the road you are on. If you see red reflectors, you should pull off the road immediately.

Budgeting and Planning

Driver Education Objectives

When driver education programs were first conceived of and put into practice the overall objective was to create in drivers a "lifetime of responsible driving." However research shows that driver education programs rarely influence a driver beyond a year's time. By this time, most drivers have become experienced and competent and are generally safe to share the road with. However, because novice drivers present such a higher accident risk, driver education objectives are beginning to shift to reduce risks during the first 6 to 12 months of driving. This goal should be attainable as this is the period when a driver education program is proven to have the most influence.

Instruction Routes

In most cases, the number of hours you are able to spend in-car with each student in a driver education program is limited. This means you must plan carefully to make the most of that time. Plan to make each in-car training session build on the last and become more challenging. In the first sessions, you should plan to choose basic routes with little traffic. Your students will be putting the theory they have learned in the classroom into practice. Take it slow at first so they can master basic skills. Once a student has learned the basic motor skills associated with driving begin introducing them into more complex driving situations. Plan your routes to expose students to a wide variety of driving situations.

Driver Education Categories

Driver education course materials can often be divided into three categories, though not all programs attempt to teach all three categories.

- First, there is basic instruction. This entails basic skills like controlling a vehicle and basic knowledge like knowing the laws and regulations in your state. Even drivers who do not participate in a driver education program must master basic skills before they can receive a license.
- Second there are safe practices. In addition to basic skills, all driver education programs should convey safe driving practices like how to drive defensively and how to identify and respond to hazards.
- Finally, there are advanced skills like learning to drive in inclement conditions, how to avoid collisions, and how to regain control of a car in a skid. Most driver education programs are not equipped to teach advanced skills.

Eligibility and Scheduling Requirements

Both the eligibility and scheduling requirements of driver education programs vary from state to state. Generally, you will find that most states allow students aged 15 years or older to participate in driver education programs. For the in-car portion of the program, most states require that students have a learner's permit. Some states issue a special permit for students participating in a driver education program that allows them to drive only when accompanied by the instructor.

Scheduling requirements in most states provide that school districts offering driver education programs must schedule classes in such a way and in such numbers as to give all eligible students an equal opportunity to enroll.

Equipment and Information Material / Methodology and Evaluation

Assessing Risk

When on the road, it is important to consider the following:

- Pay attention to the spaces around you--How close are you to other vehicles, pedestrians or other obstacles? Are you far enough to react in time should something unexpected happen? A driver must constantly observe the distances between his vehicle and his surroundings.
- Judge speeds--A driver must learn to approximate the speeds of vehicles around her, and to judge how quickly objects will cover a distance.
- Assess road conditions--If driving conditions are poor or changing, a driver must be aware and make responsible adjustments to his speed and alertness level.
- Anticipate the actions of others--Pay attention to vehicles and pedestrians. Try to predict the actions they will take. Recognize they may do something you don't expect. Be ready to react.
- Analyzes risks--As a driver you must constantly evaluate the risks around you so that you can make safe decisions.

Driving Simulations

Driving simulations help students experience driving before introducing the risks of being behind the wheel of an actual vehicle. While doing driving simulations, a student will learn to apply the lessons he or she is learning through other means in the classroom. Driving simulations help to underscore the importance of good decision-making and defensive driving. In each simulation, the student can experience a different situation and make his or her own decisions in response. The student can see the result of inappropriate decisions without danger or injury or of property damage.

Learning to make decisions and execute them is an important skill for safe, defensive driving. Driving simulations can help a student begin to develop a proper attitude of respect and responsibility toward driving. An instructor can evaluate a student's performance in a simulation and reinforce the importance of courtesy and safety while driving. The instructor can also provide immediate feedback regarding inappropriate decisions and help students to identify reactions that would have been better. Most importantly, driving simulations will help get students in the habit of making decisions and following through with them. Simulations help students learn to resolve dangerous situations safely, including situations created by improper decisions they have made.

Driving simulations help students develop their perceptual skills. Through driving simulations students will learn how to better judge speeds and distances. Because of this, they will be better able to assess a given traffic situation and respond in a safe manner. Through driving simulations students will practice basic driving skills such as changing lanes, passing another vehicle, merging into traffic and coming to a safe stop. Driving simulations also help students learn other techniques for many basic driving skills. They will learn to turn a vehicle properly, how to brake safely, how to park in variety of situations, and how to shift gears. Driving simulations help students develop good overall driving habits.

Driving simulation is the not the only tool a driving instructor needs. It will not act as the sole teaching toll and successfully relay all the knowledge a new driver needs. A driving simulation cannot replace a driver education instructor. Instead it works as a tool the helps an instructor convey the important lessons of a class. It is important that a driver education instructor underscore to his or students that the driving simulation approximates what it is like to drive a car, but does not recreate the experience exactly. Also, the driving simulation helps expose students to a variety of traffic situations, but it does not expose them to every situation possible. The most important lessons of the driving simulation are safe driving habits and how to make and execute good driving decisions.

Most driver education instruction depends on knowledge gained in the classroom and skills gained behind the wheel under the supervision of an instructor. Simulations allow students to approximate driving without submitting themselves to danger. While the primary objective of simulated driving is to help students develop perceptual skills and good driving habits, driving simulations do offer another advantage. Using a simulator, a driving instructor can expose a student both to situations that are rare and to situations that are too dangerous to actual expose a student to. These situations can help a both student and instructor see how a student will react to and handle unexpected and stressful situations.

Balanced Workload and Teaching Driver's Education

Drivers education is an important class and needs to be taken seriously by the students, parents, supervisors, and the instructor. A successful class depends on an instructor who is patient, able to tolerate error, and who understands the level of responsibility he or she must convey to the students. In-car instruction can be particularly stressful, so it is important that the driver education instructor balance the workload between in-car instruction and classroom teaching. Ideally, plan to teach a maximum of eight hours in a day between the classroom and in the car. If your day is entirely dedicated to in-car instruction, take regular breaks to avoid becoming stressed.

Methods for the Disabled

Students with disabilities are often capable of learning to be safe, competent drivers, but they may need extra assistance to learn driving skills. In the classroom portion or your instruction, consider the different learning styles of students. Some learn better from reader, some from visual instruction, and some from listening. If you have a student with a disability, contact his or her regular teacher for more information on how you can better teach them. You may find that a student needs to model demonstrated skills, may learn better from a video presentation, may find it helpful to record lessons for review, or may need to recite instructions back to you. Work with students to discover how they best learn.

Students with disabilities may need extra assistance or tailored lessons when in comes to the in-car portion of the program. It may take them longer to grasp basic driving skills. If this seems to be the case, arranging for more in-car time than usual will be beneficial. Some students may need to learn skills first in an environment free of stress. Introduce these students to basic skills in a driving course or vacant parking lot. Other student may need to master skills one part at a time. In these situations, break down an action into a series of steps. Discuss the steps, then demonstrate them in a stopped car, then in a safe environment, and finally on the road.

Observation Time

During in-car instruction it is common practice—and recommended—that one or two student observers accompany you and the student driver. The observers can receive a positive benefit from this time. They are able to observe traffic signs and other controls and varying road conditions. They are able to observe incorrect driving procedures and hear immediately how the driver education instructor corrects errors or has the student driver respond to mistakes made by other drivers. You can enhance the benefit of observation time by underscoring its importance to your students, and by asking observers questions during in-car instruction.

Car Specifics and Safety

To drive defensively you must not only see everything around you, you also have an advantage if you are easily seen. Therefore the color of your vehicle does matter. Grays and silvers make it difficult to be seen during the day, especially in the city. They tend to blend into the surrounding colors. Likewise, dark colors make it difficult to be seen at night. Give some consideration to which colors are both aesthetically pleasing and also increase your car's visibility.

Tinted windows generally reduce your ability to see clearly, so they are a poor decision for most vehicles.

Finally choose a vehicle with a lower center of gravity. It will be easier to control even in difficult situations.

Ways to Avoid Danger While Driving

When driving, it is up to you to drive defensively. Avoiding dangerous situations is key to defensive driving.

- Give large vehicle space--Follow them at a greater distance than you would other vehicles. When passing them do so at a steady speed and as quickly as is safe.
- Avoid dangerous or aggressive drivers--Recognize drivers who weave traffic, who follow too closely, or who disobey traffic laws. React to them by increasing the distance between your vehicle and theirs.
- Avoid objects in the road whenever possible--If you can, do not drive over any debris in the road. It may damage your tires or affect your control over your vehicle.
- Be wary of damaged vehicles--A vehicle that is visibly damaged may have been in a collision. This may mean that a careless driver is behind the wheel
- Drive in the outside lane--On multi-lane highways the outside lane is the safest. Use that lane unless you are passing another, slower vehicle.

Assuming the Worst

To drive defensively, you must be prepared for others to take unexpected actions. To anticipate unexpected actions, you must imagine that other drivers will make mistakes. For example, when a car in front of you has its signal on for a left turn, you should be prepared for that car to turn left, but you should also know how you will react if the car continues traveling straight ahead or if it turns right. Be prepared for vehicles not signaling to change lanes or to make turns. When coming to a stoplight, be aware of cars behind you that may not be prepared to stop. When stopped at a light that has just turned green, check that cross traffic has stopped before moving through the intersection. Never assume that another driver has seen you. Always assume that the drivers around you are paying less attention than they appear to be.

Exit Routes

The term exit route refers to the conscious decision a defensive driver makes to them him or herself somewhere to go should a collision become imminent. Avoid becoming boxed in on the freeway. Try to maintain free space to either side of you. Whenever possible, you should drive in the outside lane of the freeway. The shoulder provides and automatic exit route in most cases, and if something does happen, you will not have to cross a lane of traffic to reach the breakdown area. When driving on surface streets, also try to maintain the space on either side of you if multiple lanes travel in the same direction. When turning left at an intersection, keep your wheels pointing straight until you can actually turned. If you are rear-ended this will keep you from being knocked into the oncoming traffic lane.

Smith Method

The Smith Method of defensive driving involves five points.

- Aim High This means look ahead. Scan the road well ahead of you for obstacles and potential obstacles.
- Keep Your Eyes Moving. You should maintain awareness of the road around you in all directions including behind you. Check your mirrors, check to the side, and scan ahead.
- Get the Big Picture. Try to maintain a broad focus of what is happening around you. This will help you to anticipate the actions of others and potential hazards.
- Make Sure Others See You. Always use your headlights and signals when indicated. If a collision is imminent, make eye contact and use your horn to get the attention of other drivers.
- Leave Yourself an Out. Be aware of your exit routes. Know where you will go if it looks like another vehicle may hit you.

Humanizing Drivers

Student drivers and newly licensed drivers can introduce unique hazards to the road because of their inexperience and undeveloped sense of judgment. It is important that you as a driver education instructor teach your students proper respect for the responsibilities of driving. One way to do this is humanize all drivers of all vehicles including motorcycles and bikes. It is easy, when behind the wheel, to forget that real people are driving the vehicles around you. This can lead to aggressive behavior and road rage. By emphasizing to your students that every driver on the road is a person just like themselves and possibly someone they know, you can encourage them to drive prudently and politely.

Common Mistakes

Drivers who have only been licensed for a few months have a higher rate of automobile accidents than drivers with more experience. There are common errors that these new drivers make that lead to the higher incidence of accidents. These kinds of errors should be given particular attention in the driver education classroom. The most common mistakes that new drivers make are to allow themselves to lose their focus on the road, to fail to see upcoming hazards, to fail to properly identify hazards even when seen, and to neglect adjusting their speeds to the road conditions or to the posted speed limits.

Crash Factors

Age is the first and foremost risk factor for accidents. Teenage drivers are much more likely to have an accident that drivers in their 20s. Much of the different in accident rates can be attributed to experience, but some may be attribute to poor judgment and decisions, as well. Driving at night increases the risk of accidents, too. While driving at night increases risks for all age groups, the increase is higher among teens. Some states have responded by limiting teens to driving during the day during the first year after they have received a license. Teenagers driving with passengers double their risk of being involved in an accident. Finally, alcohol still makes a significant contribution to teenage crashes.

As a driver education instructor, it is important that you recognize the risks and behaviors that contribute to higher accident risks among newly licensed drivers. You can take steps to help mitigate these risks. First recognize the common errors made by new drivers (lack of focus, inability to recognize hazards, speeding, etc.) and give those topics proper attention in all areas of instruction. Next, explain the risks to your students so that they understand extra caution is called for in their first months of driving. Finally, underscore safe driving procedures at night and give students strategies for driving safely when teenage passengers are in the car. Also, emphasize the importance of remaining alcohol and drug free whenever students are driving.

INSTILLING SAFE HABITS

Driver education programs instill safe driving habits by imparting knowledge, teaching skills, and encouraging a proper attitude. Knowledge is information learned through instructor lectures and textbooks. Skills training gives young drivers a chance to put the classroom knowledge they have learned into practice. Skills are mastered over time through hands-on training and practice. Attitude can be the most difficult component to convey, but it may also be the most important. As a driving instructor you should attempt to teach not only a long-term attitude of responsibility, you should also impart specific beliefs that support course objectives and safe driving habits. You can do this by not only teaching students good habits but by linking those habits to the safety of the student and the people around him or her.

TRADITIONAL INSTRUCTION METHODS

In a traditional driver education program around 30 hours are spent in classroom instruction. Classroom instruction involves teacher lectures, textbook study, and video presentations. Classroom instruction can also involve question and answer sessions that allow students to delve deeper into areas that are unclear to them or bring up specific concerns. The second part of traditional instruction involves in-car instruction. Usually students spend six hours of class time behind the wheel. Many driver education vehicles are equipped with controls on the right as well as left in case the instructor needs to take over. Often students ride in the back to observe in-car instruction, providing them with additional hours to be exposed to and analyze real world driving situations.

COMPUTER TRAINING SYSTEMS

Computer-based training programs can be learner-designed. This means that they allow the student some control over the approach to learning. Computer-based training programs also provide a greater means of evaluating students' progress. The program can measure a student's reactions to instruction as well as performance. Some computer-based training programs can also offer partial simulations making driving simulations available to students who do not have access to simulators otherwise. Finally, computer-based training has proven effective in other environments and has a higher appeal to young people that a program that only involves traditional teaching methods.

WRITTEN EXAMS

Driver education instructors use written exams to measure the knowledge that students are gaining from the classroom portion of instruction. A written test will measure a student's knowledge of basic road rules, vehicle handling, and safe driving procedures. Traditionally instructors use written tests to determine if each student is learning the things necessary to become a safe driver. As a written test is also required to become a licensed driver these tests can also prepare students for that. Some experts point out that there is no correlation between doing well on a written test and becoming a safer driver, but as the knowledge of driving is essential, these tests still provide a teacher with a means of evaluation that knowledge.

In-Car Drive Tests

In most driver education programs, a student must pass only a written exam in order to pass the class. Drive tests measure practical skills and decision making, as well as driving behaviors. These tests may be more accurate and practical measures of a student's ability to be a safe driver. They may also be a better measure of whether or not you are achieving your objectives within the driver education program. Also, because states require a driving test in order to become a licensed driver, a driving test may help students better prepare to pass their licensing exams. Because a student's driving behavior under observation may differ from the behavior they exhibit when driving alone, unobtrusive methods of monitoring may be best when evaluating hands-on driving skills.

Parent's Role

Parents play an important role in teaching their teenagers how to be responsible drivers. Parents should be encouraged to actively participate in the learning process of their child. Parents can help their child become a responsible driver by helping their teenager practice driving. It is also important that parents set rules about driving. Parents should limit the number of passengers their teen can drive with as well as the times of day their teen can drive until the teen has proven driving experience. Parents should also emphasize safety rules like wearing seatbelts and obeying speed limits. Finally parents should impose consequences if their child behaves irresponsibly while driving. Driver education should encourage parents to be active in their child's driving education.

Objectives of Classroom Instruction

The objectives for classroom instruction include successfully teaching students the meaning of the gauges and lights in a car, how to safely operate a car, and the steps to go through before driving a car. Driver education programs strive to impart knowledge about traffic control devices and driving laws. They also hold among the objectives to teach students how to stop safely in a variety of situations and how to move safely around other cars. Students should also learn how natural laws affect acceleration, stopping, and turning; how to navigate hills and curves; the differences between rural, highway, and urban driving; and how to drive in adverse conditions. Student drivers also come to understand their responsibilities as a driver, how to recognize when they should not drive and what to do in an emergency.

Objectives of In-Car Portion

The objectives of the in-car portion of a driver education program are to teach students practical application of the knowledge they have been gaining in the classroom. Objectives include learning how to assess a car for safety problems before driving, what to do once in the vehicle to prepare to drive, and how to control the basic motions of the car. The objectives progress to include how to perform complex motions with the vehicle like backing up while turning and how to visually scan the road for potential hazards. The in-car portion also teaches students how to better judge stopping distances and how to manage spatial relationships. In-car teaching also helps students to recognize and practice responding to traffic control devices.

Long versus Short Blocks

When it comes to driver education, students benefit more from studying for short sessions regularly over a long period of time. This approach works better than doing long classes on the weekends, for example. Because driving is such a complex skill requiring students to engage several senses and stay broadly aware of what is happening in multiple directions, it is more effective to break the skills down into simple tasks that a student can repeat often. By doing short class periods, the instructor can focus on teaching the correct method of simple skills and build up to complex skills over time. This approach helps students to master simple skills correctly, better preparing them to handle more advanced skills.

Program Standards

Most driver education programs consider a student as successful when the student exhibits knowledge of the local driving laws. The student must also demonstrate an attitude of responsibility for his or her actions and an attitude of respect toward other drivers, pedestrians, and for the laws in general. Students must demonstrate that they understand the visual skills necessary for safe driving and that they can implement them. From a practical point of view, students must demonstrate that they can skillfully control a vehicle. They demonstrate that they understand the importance of communication to safe driving and that they can be effective communicators while driving. Students need to be able to accurately assess risk in different driving situations. Beyond all these standards of evaluation both students and instructors must understand that there is no replacement for driving experience when it comes to driving safety.

Instructor Standards

The requirements to qualify as a driver education instructor vary from state to state. In general, most states require that you have a valid teaching license within the state where you plan to teach. Some states require that you have special endorsement on your license for driver education. Many states require that you have taken a certain number of course hours in traffic safety or driver education. The course hours may require both classroom and behind-the-wheel work. Driver instructors must have a valid driver license, and usually have to submit their driving record for approval.

Behind-the-Wheel Training

During in-car lessons, you as the instructor are responsible for the safety of the student driver and any student passengers. Make sure that you choose a driving setting that matches up with the skills and confidence level of the student driver. If you are in a dual-steering vehicle, be prepared to take control at any time. If the vehicle has only driver-side steering, be prepared to take control of the steering wheel with your left hand. Make sure the student driver and all passengers have fastened their seatbelts before driving begins. Make sure both the student driver and the observer understand the objectives of the lesson. Do not allow the student driver or passengers to eat or drink during the lesson. Also, never leave students unattended in the vehicle when the motor of the car is running. Remain alert for hazards at all times and give students ample time to react to and implement your instructions.

Lesson Scheduling

Because the lessons taught in the classroom are meant to support the practical lesson taught behind-the-wheel, it is important to schedule behind-the-wheel lessons in a way that makes sense and that brings the most benefit and understanding to the students. This means that doing all the behind-the-wheel work at the end of the classroom teaching is not the best approach. Instead, in-car session should be scheduled regularly throughout the duration of the program. The focus of the behind-the-wheel sessions should directly relate to the topics most recently covered in the classroom. This integrated approach will help students correctly master the skills they need to drive safely.

Advanced Training

In novice drivers a lack of experience leads to an increased risk of accidents in the first months of driving. In an attempt to overcome the increased dangers that novice drivers take, one approach many states have taken is to offer advanced skills programs that teach things like skid control and how to drive in adverse conditions. Rather than lowering risks, some research suggests that these programs either do not change the risk of an accident for a new driver or can actually increase it. The reason is that novice drivers with advanced training often feel confidence that surpasses the actual level of their skill, which can lead them to take risks they are unprepared for. This is not to say that advanced skills training is not valuable, but that it must be balanced with an emphasis on maintaining a proper attitude of prudence while driving.

Priorities

To successfully offset a novice driver's inexperience, driver education programs must teach prudence. An instructor can do this in three ways. First the instructor must emphasize the risks that novice drivers face and underscore the cause. Doing so can encourage novice drivers to remain alert when driving and to exercise extra caution during their early months of driving. Second, a driver instructor can emphasize the driver's personal responsibility and provide new drivers with individual motivation to drive safely. No driver wants to be involved in a crash. Underscoring how poor decisions can lead to a collision can help personally motivate new drivers to drive as safely as possible. Finally, community factors play a role. If an instructor helps a new driver see how their decisions can potentially impact the community, this can help motivate the driver to be prudent.

Benefits to Other Schoolwork

Driver education program topics cross over with many other school subjects and show an immediate practical application to those subjects. For example, topics such as stopping distances, tire traction, and collision force all relate to physics. The consequences of traffic violations or drinking and driving integrate well with law and civics classes. They can cross over with health education materials, as well. By recognizing the potential for integration and using teaching materials and methods that enhance the level of integration, a driver education instructor can not only impart safe driving knowledge, but can also help students to perform better in other subjects. Peer-based teaching methods, where students interact together as they learn, can particularly enhance civics lessons.

Multi-car Range

A multi-car range is a controlled environment where student drivers can practice driving skills and begin to work on their perception of the environment around them with other moving vehicles present. The multi-car range can be a good intermediary step between classroom and behind-the-wheel training, giving student a chance to interact with other cars in a safe and more predictable environment. Because the driver education instructor does not accompany the student in the car on the multi-car range, this kind of instruction can provide the instructor a chance to observe more realistic driving behaviors in the students and address them as needed. However, multi-car range training is not a substitute for behind-the-wheel training. Eventually driving students must learn how to react to other drivers in complex and unpredictable situations.

Praxis Practice Test

1. According to the National Highway Transportation Safety Administration, which is the most common variable contributing to the majority of auto accidents?

a. Drunken driving
b. Speeding drivers
c. Driver inattention
d. Unlicensed drivers

2. Where is one *most* likely to find practice tests for the driver's license exam at no charge?

a. In a state DMV's driver manual
b. On websites offering practice tests
c. Either place is equally likely.
d. Neither of these places is likely.

3. Most states in America now place restrictions on a learner's permit or initial driver's license. These include

a. Being accompanied by a licensed adult driver
b. Only supervised driving, and only during daylight hours
c. Specified time periods with no traffic incident
d. All the above are included in learners' restrictions.

4. What does "NCDL" stand for with regard to a driver's license?

a. Non-classified driver's license
b. Non-commercial driver's license
c. Non-commissioned driver's license
d. None of the above is correct.

5. Whether commercial driver's licenses are designated as Class A, Class B, or Class C is determined by

a. The vehicle's weight limits
b. The specific type of vehicle
c. The driver's qualifications
d. The purposes of vehicle use

6. Which of the following is true about state driver's licenses and other state identification?

a. A person may have either a state driver's license or a state ID card but not both.
b. Someone not licensed to drive is required by law to have a state ID.
c. A person may have both a state driver's license and the state ID card.
d. If someone has both cards, only the license will be shown on the DMV record.

7. Which of the following statements regarding classification of driver's licenses from state to state is accurate?

a. Individual states can vary in their classification labels.
b. All classes have the exact same labels in every state.
c. Uniform labeling across all states is a federal law.
d. None of the above statements is accurate.

8. Which of the following govern(s) the use of a car horn in traffic situations?

a. Specific laws
b. Common sense
c. Both of the above
d. None of the above

9. In which of the following circumstances do most DMV driver manuals *not* advise using the car horn?

a. To warn a bicyclist heading toward a motorist's lane
b. To warn a pedestrian about to enter the street
c. To establish eye contact with another motorist
d. To alert a too-slow motorist ahead

10. In which of the following circumstances do most DMV driver manuals advise using the car horn?

a. To alert others if a driver has lost control of the vehicle
b. To express anger toward another motorist
c. To say hello to friends spotted in their cars
d. To alert blind pedestrians or horses of an approaching car

11. A 30-day window to register a vehicle does not apply

a. When the car is recently purchased
b. If the vehicle is a gift from a relative.
c. When the registration is expiring
d. If the owner has recently moved to the state

12. Which of the following documents will some drivers most likely *not* have to produce to register some vehicles?

a. A driver's license or a state ID
b. Proof of emissions inspection
c. The driver's proof of residence
d. Proof of automobile insurance

13. Which of the following is *not* true regarding titles for ownership of motor vehicles?

a. All states require and issue titles for motor vehicles.
b. Some vehicles do not require titles in some states.
c. Some states do not issue titles for vehicles.
d. None of these statements are true.

14. Which of the following is true regarding parking permits, placards, or plates for drivers with disabilities?

a. Not all states will issue these for parking.
b. Some of these are free; some have fees attached.
c. These are always free if issued.
d. All states charge a fee for issuing these.

15. Which of the following is *not* required by one of the three most basic traffic laws?

a. Obeying traffic signal lights and signs
b. Obeying police / firefighter directions
c. Not driving on officially closed roads
d. These all are requirements of the laws

16. What type of insurance is required to apply for a driver's license?

a. Liability
b. Collision
c. Comprehensive
d. All of the above

17. According to the rules of the Federal Motor Carrier Safety Administration (FMCSA), which types of drivers must carry federal motor carrier insurance with higher premiums?

a. Interstate motor carriers
b. International motor carriers
c. Hazardous materials motor carriers
d. All of the above.

18. Which of the following statements about GAP insurance is accurate?

a. It is designed only to cover a high deductible on an auto policy.
b. It pays the difference between a loan balance and the car's value.
c. It is insurance to cover the gap in Medicaid payments for prescriptions.
d. It is required in every contract when leasing an auto.

19. Which of the following is *not* true when a driver encounters a school bus on the road?

a. It is always against the law to pass any school bus.
b. It is illegal to pass a school bus when it is loading.
c. It is illegal to pass a school bus when it is unloading.
d. It is legal to pass a moving bus that doesn't have its flashers on.

20. If two drivers arrive at the same time at an intersection with no traffic lights, stop signs, or yield signs, who has the right of way?

a. The driver on the left
b. The driver on the right
c. Whoever moves first
d. They agree via signaling.

21. At an intersection with four-way stop signs, if four drivers each arrive at different times and there are no pedestrians, what is the rule for the right of way to proceed?

a. Wait for the car to the right to move even if it arrived later.
b. Wait to see who tries to proceed first before making any move.
c. Start moving immediately after a full stop to prevent confusion.
d. Whoever arrives first proceeds first, and all follow in order of arrival.

22. If a driver has the right of way at an intersection but another driver is moving out of turn, what should the first driver do?

a. Blow the horn to warn the other driver and proceed.
b. Speed up in order to get through the intersection first.
c. Let the other driver go out of turn to avoid colliding.
d. Speed up and sound the horn at the same time.

23. A driver who sees a Yield sign ahead should

a. Slow down and be prepared to stop if necessary
b. Continue at speed if no obstacles are in sight
c. Immediately hit the brakes and make a full stop
d. Look to see who is coming before slowing down

24. To which of the following would a driver turning left *not* yield the right of way?

a. All traffic going any direction when turning left at an intersection
b. All oncoming traffic when turning left at an intersection
c. All oncoming traffic when turning left into a driveway
d. All oncoming traffic when turning left into an alleyway

25. Which of the following statements is incorrect regarding a driver who has the green light at an intersection with traffic?

a. The driver should wait until the intersection is clear of all traffic.
b. The driver should wait until no traffic is nearing the intersection.
c. The driver should proceed right away because he has the green light.
d. None of the above

26. If traffic is merging onto the road or highway, a driver already on the road should

a. Change lanes
b. Speed up
c. Slow down
d. Any of the above

27. If a police car, a fire engine, an ambulance, or other emergency service vehicles are on the road using sirens and flashing lights, a driver should

a. Pull over to the right shoulder of the road and stop
b. Pull as far as possible to the right and stop
c. Pull over, stop; do not block intersections or turns
d. Do all of the above in so far as possible

28. Which of the following statements about making a "right turn on red" at a red light is incorrect?

a. It is permitted after having made a complete stop.
b. It is permitted only where a sign is posted stating so.
c. It is legal after yielding to all traffic and pedestrians.
d. It is permitted after making sure it can be done safely.

29. Which of the following statements about making a left turn at a red light is incorrect?

a. It is never allowed to turn left at a red light.
b. It is allowed going between one-way roads.
c. It is allowed from left lanes into left traffic.
d. It is allowed if (b) and (c) are both the case.

30. On a two-lane road, a driver may pass another vehicle

a. Wherever it may be safely done
b. Where a solid yellow line is right of center
c. Where broken lines are right of center.
d. Wherever there are double yellow lines

31. A motorist who has passed another car on its left on a two-lane road must return to the right lane before

a. The passing zone ends
b. Entering an intersection
c. Oncoming cars are close
d. All of the above

32. After passing a car to its left on a two-lane road, a motorist must return to the right lane before any oncoming traffic is within __ feet of his car.

a. 100
b. 200
c. 300
d. 500

33. Which of the following is true about "blind spots" when driving?

a. All drivers have a blind spot where they cannot see what is behind and to the side.
b. Only some drivers have blind spots, but these should always be taken into account.
c. Only those driving very large, tall vehicles like trucks will have a true "blind spot."
d. The "blind spot" is eliminated by having side-view mirrors on both sides of the car.

34. After passing a car to its left, a driver should return to the right lane

a. As soon and as quickly as possible
b. After clearing the other car by three car lengths
c. After the other car's headlights are visible in the rear-view mirror
d. After the other driver has signaled that it's alright

35. Passing on a two-lane road is not allowed within 100 feet of

a. A railroad crossing
b. A bridge or tunnel
c. Any intersections
d. Any or all of the above

36. What is a (usually bright white) line painted along the right side of the road called?

a. Shoulder line
b. Road line
c. Fog line
d. White line

37. Which of the following statements is *not* true about the vehicle used for taking the road test for a driver's license?

a. The applicant being tested must provide the vehicle.
b. The vehicle is required to have turn signal indicators.
c. The vehicle must be covered by liability insurance.
d. The vehicle to be used must pass a safety inspection.

38. Which of the following statements is *not* correct about cars in driver's license road tests?

a. There is no accepted substitute for a valid registered license plate.
b. A bill of sale/proof of purchase can be used with a recently bought car.
c. A rental can be used, if the applicant shows the contract and is listed on it.
d. Proof of insurance is required for a rental car the same as any other.

39. If an applicant has scheduled an appointment for the driver's license road test but there is a terrible thunderstorm at the time, which of the following would happen?

a. The applicant would take the road test anyway because storms occur in real life.
b. The applicant would take the test, but the examiner would make allowances for weather.
c. The applicant would have to wait a specified time before rescheduling.
d. The applicant would reschedule the appointment; the test must be safe for both the examiner and the applicant.

40. Which of the following is *not* normally tested during a driver's license road test?

a. Parallel parking along a curb
b. Parking within a parking lot
c. Safely making a quick stop
d. Backing up over a distance

41. Which of the following is *not* a part of the driver's license road test?

a. Smooth accelerations
b. Stopping for traffic signs/lights
c. Two-, three-, or four-point turns
d. Correctly yielding right of way

42. To pass a road test and when driving in real life, which of the following applies to turning corners?

a. Drivers must be in the correct lane before arriving at the corner.
b. Drivers must signal a turn far enough ahead of a corner.
c. Drivers must look in both directions before turning.
d. All of the above

43. A road test examiner will determine that a driver is following too closely if it takes less than _ seconds for the vehicle to reach the same place as the car in front.

a. One
b. Two
c. Three
d. Five

44. Which of the following is true about driving a car with a manual transmission for the road test?

a. The examiner must be certified to test with manual transmissions.
b. An applicant who drives one must also be tested on an automatic transmission.
c. The applicant must be able to shift gears smoothly and correctly.
d. An applicant's driving will be tested but not specifically how he shifts the gears.

45. Jack did not score enough points on his road test to pass. Which of the following actions would have had a negative impact on his score?

a. He leaned his left elbow on the edge of the open window while driving.
b. He made small talk with the examiner in hope of establishing a rapport.
c. He passed another vehicle after checking behind his own car for safety.
d. (d) Any of the above

46. Which of the following will not differ between road tests for non-commercial and commercial driver's licenses?

a. Passing the safety inspection
b. Gross vehicle weight rating
c. The minimum passing score
d. None of the above would differ.

47. Complete the following sentence: A motorist on a multi-lane highway may pass a motorcyclist

a. On the left side only
b. On the right side only
c. From an adjacent lane
d. In the same lane if there is room

48. Which of the following automotive parts would *not* be involved if a driver has trouble stopping?

a. A master cylinder
b. A caliper/calipers
c. A set of struts
d. A solenoid cell

49. Stacy's car did not pass its emissions inspection. The mechanic told her she needed to have a certain part replaced for it to pass. Which part would *not* be the likely one?

a. Catalytic converter
b. Alternator
c. Exhaust pipe
d. EGR valve

50. Which of these is *not* a method designed to promote safe defensive driving?

a. The SIPDE Process
b. The Smith System
c. The Zone System
d. Zone control system

51. Complete the following sentence: Flashing the turn signal to notify a following driver that it's OK to pass is

a. Illegal
b. Only a courtesy
c. Required by law
d. None of the above

52. When parallel parking correctly, how far should a car be from the curb?

a. 12 inches
b. 18 inches
c. 24 inches
d. 36 inches

53. Eric skillfully drives a Porsche and constantly switches lanes on the highway in order to pass all other vehicles without slowing down. What can most accurately be said about his behavior?

a. Eric's driving is risky but not illegal.
b. Eric's driving is inconsiderate but safe.
c. Eric's skill and car warrant his actions.
d. Eric's practice of weaving is unlawful.

54. A sign alerting motorists to highway construction would *not* be:

a. A yellow diamond
b. An orange diamond
c. An orange rectangle
d. Any of the above

55. Where is a driver never allowed to stop, stand, or park a motor vehicle?

a. On a sidewalk
b. In a crosswalk
c. In an intersection
d. All of the above

56. A driver who has to stop, stand, or park a motor vehicle for a short time to pick up or drop off passengers must be the farthest away from which of the following?

a. A fire hydrant
b. A railroad crossing
c. A traffic control signal
d. A fire station driveway

57. Where should a U-turn *not* be made?

a. At a No U-turn sign
b. On a curve in the road
c. Near the top of a hill
d. In any of the above scenarios

58. Which of the following is *not* true about maximum speed limits for driving?

a. They are uniformly set by the federal government.
b. They vary among urban, suburban and rural roads.
c. They can vary from state to state.
d. None of the above applies to maximum speed limits.

59. When conditions dictate that a driver must stop before a railroad crossing, how far away from the tracks should he be?

a. More than 50 feet away.
b. More than 15 feet away.
c. Less than 15 feet away.
d. At least 10 feet away.

60. A driver is always required to stop before a railroad crossing when

a. The crossing gates are lowered
b. The railroad signal is flashing
c. Either of the above is true.
d. Neither of the above is the case.

61. Drivers must always stop before a railroad crossing if

a. A flagman is giving the signal for cars to stop
b. The train itself is giving cars a warning signal
c. Neither of the above always means cars must stop.
d. Each of the above always means cars must stop.

62. Which of the following is *not* true about highway/street construction or maintenance work zones?

a. More than half of all road workers' deaths are caused by motor vehicles.
b. One-third of worker deaths by vehicles are from intrusion into work zones.
c. Two-thirds of all road workers are killed by motor vehicles in work zones.
d. None of these statements is true about deaths in road work zones.

63. Which of the following situations is *not* defined as a highway or road work zone?

a. People working on power lines above roads
b. People working to remove snow from roads
c. Surveyors measuring land near the road
d. All of the above are defined as road work zones.

64. Which of the following statements is *not* correct about speed limits in road work zones?

a. Speed limits may be slower or the same as usually posted in a road work zone.
b. Speed limits are always slower than the usual in work zones.
c. Violating the posted speed limit in a work zone can incur a fine.
d. Breaking the speed limit in work zones can incur prison time.

65. Which of the following is *not* a valid tip given by state driver manuals for driving in road work zones?

a. Drivers should try to change to lanes away from the road work.
b. Expect the unexpected in a work zone and prepare for it.
c. It is not necessary to slow down when entering a work zone.
d. Fines for disobeying work zone speed limits are usually higher than elsewhere.

66. Which of the following statements about drinking and driving is true?

a. A driver who is less than 21 years of age is classified as intoxicated if he has blood alcohol of greater than 0.02 percent by weight.
b. A driver who is at least 21 years of age is classified as intoxicated if he has blood alcohol of greater than 0.02 percent by weight.
c. A driver who is at least 21 years of age is classified as intoxicated if he has blood alcohol of greater than 0.08 percent by weight.
d. A driver who is less than 21 years of age is classified as intoxicated if he has any measurable amount of alcohol in his blood.

67. What is true about driving while taking prescription medications?

a. Having a prescription is not a defense if the drug impairs the ability to drive.
b. The laws for illegal drugs are the same as for alcohol but not for legal drugs.
c. The laws for legal and illegal drugs are different from those governing alcohol.
d. If a driver is prescribed a drug necessary to health, the laws no longer apply.

68. Aggressive driving is considered operating a motor vehicle with the intent to

a. Annoy or harass another person
b. Molest or intimidate another person
c. Injure or obstruct another person
d. Do any of the above to another person

69. Which penalty for driving aggressively applies specifically to drivers under 21 years of age?

a. Punishment by assessment of a fine
b. Punishment by a prison sentence
c. Suspension of all driving privileges
d. All of the above apply specifically to drivers under 21.

70. Which of the following is *not* true regarding reckless driving?

a. Penalties for driving recklessly include being fined.
b. Reckless driving is the same as aggressive driving.
c. Penalties for driving recklessly can include prison time.
d. Penalty for reckless drivers under 21 is suspension of driving privileges.

71. Which of the following statements about driving or parking near moving or stopped emergency vehicles or apparatus responding to fire alarms is correct?

a. The distance for following any moving emergency vehicles/apparatus is 200 feet or more.
b. The distance for parking near stopped emergency vehicles/apparatus is 200 feet or more.
c. The distance for following any moving emergency vehicles/apparatus is 500 feet or more.
d. The distance given in none of the above statements is correct.

72. Which of the following statements about vehicles pulling trailers on roads outside of business or residential districts is *most* accurate?

a. Drivers of such vehicles are encouraged to form caravans in the same lane.
b. Drivers of such vehicles are discouraged from forming caravans in the same lane.
c. It is unlawful for vehicles pulling trailers to engage in "caravanning."
d. It is unnecessary to leave space for other vehicles if pulling a trailer.

73. Which of the following statements regarding riding in vehicle-drawn trailers is *not* true?

a. It is illegal to ride in a trailer being pulled by a vehicle.
b. Laws differ for riding in house trailers or horse trailers.
c. Having no seat-belt restraint in a trailer is a hazard for a rider.
d. Possible separation of trailer from vehicle is a hazard.

74. Which of the following is *not* true when driving a motor vehicle?

a. Using a hand-held cell phone while driving is illegal in some states.
b. It is illegal to wear anything that can impair hearing.
c. Wearing a hands-free Bluetooth device is allowed.
d. Wearing headsets or headphones is against the law.

75. Which of the following situations is *least* likely to violate a law while driving a motor vehicle?

a. Wearing corrective lenses which are needed but not specified on one's license
b. Driving with a human child, adult, or animal on one's lap
c. Driving while wearing sunglasses at night or in the dark
d. Driving a car piled with objects/materials all around the interior

76. In North America, Australia, and New Zealand, which type of sign would *not* be red with white letters/symbols?

a. A stop sign
b. A yield sign
c. A no parking sign
d. A school zone sign

77. Where are standardized road signs or markers found in the United States?

a. Local roads
b. County markers
c. Federal highways
d. State highways

78. In the United States, the color orange with black letters/symbols is used for

a. Detour signs
b. Road construction
c. Temporary traffic control zones
d. All of the above

79. In the United States, green signs with white are *not* used for

a. Historical sites
b. Naming locations
c. Giving mile distances
d. Directional information

80. What color scheme is used for signs to campgrounds in the United States?

a. Blue with white
b. Brown with white
c. White with black
d. Yellow with black

81. In the United States, a sign that is brown with white letters would *not* indicate

a. A park
b. A ski area
c. A rest area
d. A forest

82. How many sides does a US stop sign have?

a. Eight
b. Six
c. Four
d. Three

83. A pentagonal sign is likely to show

a. A hazard warning
b. A school crossing
c. A railroad crossing
d. The need to yield

84. In Australia, road signs indicating kangaroo crossings are common (similar to deer-crossing signs on American roads). They will show a black silhouette of a hopping kangaroo. What shape is this sign likely to be?

a. Round
b. Diamond
c. Triangular
d. Rectangular

85. A sign indicating Thru Traffic would be which shape?

a. A vertical rectangle
b. A horizontal rectangle
c. A diamond
d. A triangle

86. A sign that says No Parking in red or black letters on a vertical white rectangle

a. Must be obeyed as a traffic law
b. Is a suggestion, not a traffic law
c. Must be obeyed only if it is red
d. Varies in legality from place to place

87. When is a purple road sign used in the United States?

a. There is no such thing as a purple road sign in the United States.
b. Purple is sometimes used on incident management signs.
c. Purple indicates lanes for vehicles with electronic toll accounts.
d. Purple is a nonstandard color sometimes used on detour signs.

88. Which of the following is *not* true about languages used on road signs?

a. Road signs in the United States and Canada may have 1, 2, or 3 languages.
b. All road signs in the United States use the English language only.
c. Certain locations in Canada and the United States have bilingual road signs.
d. Canada mostly uses English signs but has French signs in Québec.

89. In Israel, many road signs are in which of these languages?

a. Hebrew
b. Arabic
c. English
d. All of the above

90. Which of the following is not an alternative color used today for road signs in many parts of the United States?

a. Fluorescent pink
b. Fluorescent green
c. Fluorescent yellow
d. Fluorescent orange

91. Which of the following would not be classified as a regulatory sign?

a. Do Not Enter
b. Two-Way Traffic
c. Wrong Way
d. One Way

92. Which of the following is true about hydroplaning?

a. A driver cannot brake, accelerate, or steer when hydroplaning.
b. It is defined as plowing through standing water with car tires on the road.
c. It is defined as operating an airplane atop or above the water.
d. It means driving on a plane/surface that is under deep water.

93. A driver who begins to skid on a slippery surface should

a. Yank his foot off the gas pedal
b. Stomp on the brakes immediately
c. Steer the car away from the skid
d. Steer the car in the skid direction

94. Which answer does not correctly complete the following statement? Generally, it can take up to __ feet to stop a vehicle from a speed of _ mph.

a. 100; 30
b. 200; 40
c. 400; 60
d. 600; 80

95. Which of the following statements is *not* true about the probability of death to a pedestrian if struck by a motor vehicle traveling at any of the following speeds?

a. The chances of fatality are less than 10% if the vehicle was going 20 mph.
b. The chances of fatality are less than 60% if the vehicle was going 40 mph.
c. The chances of fatality are less than 50% if the vehicle was going 30 mph.
d. The chances of fatality are greater than 70% if the vehicle was going 40 mph.

96. Which of the following is correct regarding median strips in roadways?

a. Driving across a median is frowned on but not illegal.
b. Driving on a median is allowed only in emergencies.
c. Only authorized openings or turnarounds can be used.
d. Drivers are encouraged to use the median to avoid a collision.

97. If a person in a parked car opened the door and it was struck by a moving vehicle in the adjacent lane, who would be at fault, according to the law?

a. The driver of the moving vehicle
b. The person who opened the car door into traffic
c. Fault would be determined by a police officer or judge.
d. The person in the parked car and the other driver would be equally at fault.

98. Which of the following is *not* true about driving the wrong way on a one-way street?

a. It is permitted by police vehicles when necessary.
b. Authorized emergency vehicles may do so when necessary.
c. Drivers may do so if directed by construction or emergency staff.
d. If a traffic control device directs drivers to do so, it is nonetheless illegal.

99. Which of the following is not a warning sign?

a. Merge
b. Keep Right
c. Signal Ahead
d. No Passing Zone

100. What is the standard position of the green light in a traffic signal?

a. On the top
b. In the middle
c. On the bottom
d. There is no standard.

Answer Key

Question	Answer	Question	Answer	Question	Answer	Question	Answer
1	C	26	D	51	A	76	D
2	A	27	D	52	B	77	C
3	D	28	B	53	D	78	D
4	B	29	A	54	A	79	A
5	A	30	C	55	D	80	B
6	C	31	D	56	B	81	C
7	A	32	B	57	D	82	A
8	B	33	A	58	A	83	B
9	D	34	C	59	B	84	B
10	A	35	D	60	C	85	B
11	C	36	C	61	D	86	A
12	B	37	B	62	C	87	C
13	A	38	A	63	D	88	B
14	B	39	D	64	B	89	D
15	D	40	B	65	C	90	C
16	A	41	A	66	C	91	B
17	D	42	D	67	A	92	A
18	B	43	B	68	D	93	D
19	A	44	C	69	C	94	A
20	B	45	D	70	B	95	B
21	D	46	A	71	A	96	C
22	C	47	C	72	C	97	B
23	A	48	D	73	B	98	D
24	A	49	B	74	C	99	B
25	C	50	C	75	A	100	C

Answer Explanations

1. C: According to the National Highway Transportation Safety Administration, the leading contributor to most auto accidents is (c) driver inattention, which causes more accidents than drunken driving (a), speeding drivers (b), or unlicensed drivers (d). Distraction of drivers' attention is caused by such things as using cell phones for conversations; sending and receiving text messages, and playing overly loud music while driving.

2. A: One is *most* likely to find practice tests for the driver's license exam at no charge (a) in a state Department of Motor Vehicles (DMV)'s driver manual, normally available in hard copy or online. Websites offering practice tests (b) typically charge a fee for the tests (for example, $14.95 for 100 questions and answers). Therefore, finding *free* sample questions is not equally likely at either place (c). Because practice tests are most likely to be found in a state DMV's driver manual or handbook; the answer (d), neither of these, is incorrect.

3. D: While state laws vary, most states do impose restrictions on the learner's license/permit. For example, in many states, a learning driver initially must drive only during daylight hours (b) with a licensed adult driver (a). Those with learner's licenses must drive with no incidents for a specified time period (c) before being permitted to drive at night. These restrictions all apply to learning drivers (d), which is the correct answer. The learner also may need to supply documentation and approval of a specified number of hours of practice driving.

4. B: NCDL stands for non-commercial driver's license, which is another term for a standard driver's license. This is the most commonly issued license for drivers of passenger cars that are not taxicabs, limousines, or other cars used for business purposes. NCDL does not stand for non-classified (a) or non-commissioned (c) with regard to driver's licenses. Because (b) is correct, answer (d), none of the above, is incorrect.

5. A: Class A, Class B, and Class C are classifications of commercial driver's licenses. The class is determined by (a) the vehicle's weight limits. For example, a Class A commercial license permits transportation of vehicles weighing 26,001 pounds and towing of trailers weighing more than 10,001 pounds. These classifications are made not according to the vehicle's specific type (b) but its weight. Neither are they determined by the driver's qualifications (c), although, of course, the driver must be qualified to drive the class of vehicles with its weight limits. Because the classes are determined by weight, the purpose(s) for which the vehicle is used (d) does not affect the vehicle's classification.

6. C: A person can have both a driver's license and a state ID card. It is not true that someone cannot have both (a) at the same time. Neither is it true that a person is required by law to have a state ID if he isn't licensed to drive (b). People without driver's licenses may find it helpful to obtain a state ID card because it is accepted in lieu of a driver's license for identification purposes only (not as a license to drive). However, this is an individual's choice. The law does not require anyone to get a state ID. It also is not true that if a person has both cards, only the driver's license will show on the DMV record (d). Both cards will show on the DMV record if someone has both. The state ID will be listed there as "ID Card" under the heading for class of license.

7. A: Individual states may vary in the labels they use to classify driver's licenses. Thus it is not true that all classes are labeled exactly the same in each state (b) or that uniform labeling across states is a federal law (c). Because (a) is accurate, answer (d), none of the above statements is accurate, is incorrect.

8. B: The proper use of a car horn is governed by (b) common sense and not by (a) specific legislation. Therefore, both of the above (c) does not apply. Because common sense does apply, neither of the above (d) is also incorrect.

9. D: Most DMV manuals do not advise sounding the car horn (d) to alert a motorist driving too slowly ahead. "Too slowly" is a subjective phrase and usually refers not to someone going far below the speed limit but to someone going slower than the driver behind him/her would like. Even if the driver ahead is going far below the speed limit, it is up to a police officer to determine if the driver is going "dangerously" slowly. It is not considered proper horn use to beep at another driver out of impatience. If the driver is having car trouble, he cannot speed up. Even if the horn is used to alert the driver, it likely will only scare him instead. Most DMV manuals do advise using the horn to warn a bicyclist who is straying into a driver's lane (a) to move so he doesn't get hit; to warn pedestrians about to enter the street (b) or road, so they, likewise, are not struck by a vehicle, or to make eye contact with and get another motorist's attention (c) for various traffic-related reasons, e.g., getting or giving an OK to change lanes, etc.

10. A: Of the choices listed here, most DMV manuals advise using the car horn only to alert others when a driver has lost control of the car. (a). In this situation the horn would warn others that the out-of-control vehicle may hit other cars and/or pedestrians and the driver may not be able to steer or brake to avoid them. It is not recommended in most DMV manuals to blow the horn to display anger toward another driver (b), although some motorists often do so. Horns should be used as warnings or to alert others, not to vent hostility. They should not be used to greet friends driving in another lane (c), either. This can distract both drivers and can be misinterpreted by others as a warning, an alert, or angry honking, causing confusion and reducing safety. Neither should one use the horn around blind pedestrians or horses (d), because both will be unduly frightened by it.

11. C: A 30-day window to register a vehicle would not apply to (c). It would apply to a recently purchased vehicle (a), a vehicle for which ownership is being transferred (b), or to register a vehicle after a recent move to another state (d). A vehicle does not need to be registered if its current registration is going to expire (c); in that case, the registration would be renewed rather than registering the vehicle for the first time.

12. B: The most likely documentation that some drivers will be exempt from producing is (b) proof of a passed emissions inspection. Some vehicles are not required to have emissions inspections. To register a vehicle, drivers must produce their driver's license or state ID (a), proof of their residence (c), and proof of valid automobile insurance for the vehicle (d).

13. A: It is not true that all states require and issue titles for motor vehicles (a). In some states, certain types of vehicles do not require titling (b). Moreover, some states do not issue titles (c). Because (b) and (c) are true, answer (d), none of the statements are true, is incorrect.

14. B: The only true choice is (b): Some disabled parking permits are free and some have fees attached. Applications for disabled parking permits include a section to be completed by a physician to identify the applicant's disability and to certify whether it is temporary or permanent. All states will issue such parking permits, so (a) is not true. Because some permits are free and some carry a fee, answers (c) and (d) are both incorrect.

15. D: These all are requirements (d). The three most basic traffic laws include (a) obeying traffic lights and signs; (b) obeying traffic directions when given by police officers or firefighters, even if they conflict with existing traffic lights or signs; and (c) refraining from driving onto roadways officially closed for construction, a special public event, or any other reason.

16. A: Liability insurance (a) is required by law to obtain a license and to drive. This means that if a person is found legally liable for a motor vehicle accident, his insurance will pay for the other party's damages, i.e., bodily injury and property damage. Collision (b) insurance is not legally required for a driver's license. It covers damages and loss to the insured's vehicle in the event of collision with other vehicles, obstructions in the road, stationary objects and such. Collision insurance is indicated if a vehicle is new, i.e., the value of the vehicle is more than the cost of the insurance, and/or the owner can afford such insurance. Comprehensive insurance (c) covers damages and loss to a vehicle from virtually anything that could happen besides collision, such as theft, flooding, fire, hail, vandalism, etc. This type of insurance, like collision, is to benefit the owner if the vehicle is worth enough to warrant the premium price, but it is not required by law for licensed driving. If a loan was taken out to buy a vehicle, comprehensive insurance, including fire and theft coverage, may be required by the lender. Because only (a) is correct, answer (d), all of the above, is incorrect.

17. D: All of the drivers listed must have federal motor carrier insurance (d). Those with commercial-class driver's licenses who transport cargo across state lines (a); who transport cargo across more than one country (b); and who transport hazardous materials (c) must carry this insurance, which has premiums higher than those of standard motor vehicle insurance. Employees found driving without proof of this insurance can set off a federal investigation of the company's record-keeping and inspection of all company vehicles. The absence of such insurance also can incur federal and state fines and even loss of the driver's commercial driver's license.

18. B: The only accurate statement is (b): GAP--Guaranteed Auto Protection--insurance is designed to help cover the gap between how much is owed on a car loan or leased vehicle and how much the vehicle actually is worth. A new vehicle's value is depreciated as soon as the vehicle is driven. In the event of a loss, the auto insurance policy pays the depreciated value; it's possible that the owner would not receive as much benefit from the insurance provider as he still owes for the vehicle. GAP insurance helps bridge this shortfall, which can be a significant amount if the vehicle was purchased recently, the down payment was small, and the loan carries interest. This insurance is not only for covering a high deductible on an auto policy (a), although in some cases its payout may indeed cover the deductible amount. GAP insurance is designed to cover whatever is not paid by a driver's primary auto insurance. It refers to auto insurance, not to insurance to cover the gap in Medicaid Part D payments for prescription drugs (c). This "gap" in coverage is more commonly referred to as the "doughnut hole," which current health insurance reform legislation aims to eliminate in coming years. Not all leasing contracts require GAP insurance (d), although many companies do include such a requirement in their contracts. Some will offer GAP insurance themselves for a fee by including it in the contract. Many companies do so because with leasing, as with a loan, a customer can take a long time to repay the vehicle's value to the company, and this insurance will help the borrower pay back that value in the event of a wreck, theft, or other loss. However, GAP insurance, while a good idea with certain car loans or leases, is not always required in every contract.

19. A: It is not always illegal to pass any school bus (a). When a school bus stops to unload passengers, its lights flash yellow, at which point all motorists in the vicinity should slow down, be ready to stop, and be observant for any children walking across or along the road. When the flashing lights change from yellow to red and the bus's stop signs extend, children will be getting on or off the bus; it is illegal to pass the bus when it is loading (b) or unloading (c) children. It is not against the law to pass a moving school bus that is driving on the road with no flashing lights (d) because the bus is not stopped and children are not getting on or off it.

20. B: When two vehicles arrive simultaneously at an intersection without traffic signals, stop signs or yield signs, the driver of the vehicle on the right (b) has the right of way. The driver of the vehicle on the left (a) does not and should yield the right of way to the car on the right. This rule is governed by the location of the vehicles and not by whoever decides to proceed first (c), a driving error that causes many accidents. Neither is it lawful nor a good idea to signal to one another to agree (d) who should proceed first. The driver on the right has the right of way, and the driver on the left must yield.

21. D: The rule in this case is (d): Whoever arrived at the intersection first proceeds first after making a full stop; whoever arrived second proceeds second after the full stop, and so forth in the same order of arrival. It is not correct to wait for the car on the right to move even if it arrived later (a). A driver would yield to the car on its right if both cars arrived at the intersection at the same time. It is not correct to wait to see who tries to go first before moving (b). Of course, if another motorist is not following the rule and his vehicle is already moving, it is common sense not to proceed and collide with that vehicle; this is defensive driving. But sitting and waiting when no other car is moving is overly defensive and can be dangerous by misleading other drivers, just as barging ahead (c) is dangerous. All four drivers should not start moving immediately after making a full stop to "prevent confusion" because all four do not have the right of way. The car that arrived first has the right to proceed first after the full stop, but that car's driver should look to make sure that another driver or drivers are not ignoring his right of way and moving prematurely.

22. C: If a driver takes another's turn at an intersection even though he does not have the right of way, the first driver should (c) let that driver proceed because this can prevent a collision. The fact that the other driver is proceeding before the first driver without having the right of way indicates that this driver either does not know or does not care who has the right of way. Insisting on what is lawful is of no benefit if someone is killed, injured, or loses the use of their car, etc., due to a collision. Safety and common sense override the law if the other motorist is not following it. Blowing the horn while proceeding (a) is no guarantee the other driver will stop or slow down and can still result in a collision. Speeding up to get through the intersection before the other driver (b) is not a safe choice. The increased speed will only make the ensuing collision worse if the driver doesn't get past the other car. Also, speeding up suddenly could cause an accident involving other cars and/or pedestrians. Speeding up while sounding the horn (d) will not necessarily stop the other driver, either, and will likely cause an accident.

23. A: When approaching a Yield sign, a driver should (a) slow down and be prepared to stop if necessary. If it is necessary to stop, a driver should not proceed until it is safe to do so. A Yield sign does not mean a driver should continue at the same speed if nothing is in sight (b). This would not allow the driver to stop if necessary. A Yield sign is not a Stop sign; drivers should not immediately hit the brakes for a full stop (c) when nearing a Yield sign. This could cause a following motorist to rear-end the stopped car. Looking to see who is coming before slowing down (d) is not safe or practical because it may not allow the driver to slow down in time, and it is harder to look when going at higher speeds. Slowing down first allows a driver to look and also to stop if needed.

24. A: A driver would not yield the right of way to (a) all traffic going in any direction when turning left at an intersection. Motorists must yield the right of way to all oncoming traffic—that is, all traffic coming from the opposite direction--when turning left at an intersection (b). Motorists also must yield the right of way to all oncoming traffic when turning left into a driveway (c) or an alley (d).

25. C: The wrong choice is (c): If the intersection is full of traffic, a driver should not proceed right away just because he has the green light. Drivers should wait until the traffic has cleared from the intersection (a). They also should wait until no traffic is immediately approaching the intersection (b). Even though the green light gives the right of way, an accident could result if another car approaching the intersection reaches it at the same time. Because only (c) is wrong and (a) and (b) are right, answer (d), none of the above, is incorrect.

26. D: A driver on a highway where traffic is merging should do any of these (d) depending on the circumstances. The first option should be to change lanes (a) away from the merging traffic if possible. If changing lanes is impossible, the driver should adjust vehicle speed either by going faster (b) or slower (c) to allow traffic to merge safely without a collision—either between his car and merging vehicles; between or among merging vehicles when his car is in the way, or between or among his car and others as a result of attempts to get out of the way of merging traffic.

27. D: If an emergency service vehicle is using its siren and flashing lights, a driver should (d) do all of the above in so far as possible. If possible, a driver should pull over to the right shoulder of the road and stop (a). If this is impossible due to traffic and/or a road with no shoulder, drivers should pull as far as possible to the right and stop (b). When pulling over, drivers must be sure not to block intersections or other turns (c) that an emergency vehicle may need to travel through. Of course, when pulling over and stopping for emergency vehicles, one should always watch out for pedestrians, cyclists, and other motor vehicles.

28. B: The incorrect choice is that "right turn on red" is permitted only where a sign is posted stating so (b). There does not need to be a sign stating this. However, right turns on red are not permitted where a sign is posted stating "No turn on red." If no sign prohibiting a right turn on red is posted, the turn is permitted after first making a complete stop (a), yielding to all other traffic and pedestrians (c), and making sure the turn can be completed safely (d). All three correct choices are required before making such a turn.

29. A: The incorrect choice is that it is never allowed to turn left at a red light (a). A "left turn on red" is allowed when turning from a one-way road to another one-way road (b); when turning from the left lane onto a road with traffic going to the left (c); and only if both of these are the case (d). As with a "right turn on red," the left turn on red should be made only after making a complete stop, yielding to all other traffic and pedestrians, and making sure the turn can be completed safely.

30. C: On a two-lane road, a driver may pass another vehicle (c) where there is a broken (or dashed or striped) line to the right of the center line. The broken line designates a passing zone. A driver may not pass wherever it may be safely done (a) but only in a marked passing zone. A solid yellow line to the right of the center line (b) indicates passing is not permitted. Neither is passing permitted where there are double yellow lines (d). Of course, one may not pass wherever a sign states Do Not Pass.

31. D: When passing on the left on a two-lane road, a motorist must return to the right lane before the marked passing zone has ended (a); before coming into an intersection (b), and before oncoming cars are too close (c). The correct answer, therefore, is (d) all of the above.

32. B: After passing to the left on a two-lane road, a motorist must return to the right lane before any oncoming traffic is within (b) 200 feet of his car. This is considered a safe distance to avoid collisions or dangerous evasive maneuvers. Answer (a), 100 feet, is not far enough when cars may be going 55 mph or faster. Three hundred feet (c) is farther than necessary or practicable. And 500 feet (d) is too far away at normal speeds and would be difficult to accomplish.

33. A: All drivers have a blind spot, typically behind and to either side, where they cannot see a vehicle, object or person near their car (a). That is why it is necessary at times to turn and look around before executing certain maneuvers (e.g. turning, changing lanes, backing up, etc.). It is not true that only some drivers have blind spots (b). The blind spot is not due to an individual's vision or perception but to the position of the unseen object combined with the size and shape of the vehicle and the location and position of the driver. As such, a blind spot will always exist until or unless the driver changes position. It is not true that only drivers of large, high trucks have blind spots (c). Theirs will simply be in a different area from the blind spot of drivers in smaller cars. Neither is it true that the blind spot is eliminated by having both left- and right-side view mirrors (d). These afford the driver more vision of what is behind on the right, but there will still be a spot that cannot be seen without physically turning and looking. Drivers are always advised to look behind them when backing up their vehicle.

34. C: After passing on the left, a driver should return to the right lane when the headlights of the passed car are visible in the rear-view mirror (c). This indicates the driver is far enough ahead of the passed car to avoid a collision, which also is why the driver should not move back into the right lane immediately or as soon and as quickly as possible (a). Waiting until clearing the other car by three car lengths (b) is farther than necessary and also difficult to gauge while driving. No law, rule, courtesy or convention dictates that the other driver is to signal it's all right (d) to move back in front of his car after passing it. (Some drivers will wave after passing and *after* moving back in front of another car as a courtesy, to thank the other driver for allowing them to pass, or to acknowledge that they are finished changing lanes, and some other drivers will wave back in response, but this is never required.)

35. D: It is illegal to pass on a two-lane road within 100 feet of (d): any or all of the above, which includes: (a) a railroad crossing; (b) a bridge or a tunnel; (c) any intersections, and also within 100 feet of a viaduct. Other conditions under which passing is not allowed within 100 feet include when school buses are loading or unloading, when a solid yellow line is to the right of the center line, double yellow lines, a Do Not Pass sign, when there is oncoming traffic, on hills or curves with limited visibility, or on the shoulder of the road.

36. C: A line, usually white, painted along the right side of the road is called a (c) fog line. This term originated from areas that get heavy fog, where such lines are painted on roads with no curbs, highways with no retaining walls, etc., to help motorists see the edge of the road and not drive off it when visibility is poor. These days, bike routes lie beyond the fog line along some roads. Shoulder line (a) and white line (d) are descriptors, not actual names, of this line, and road line (b) is too general and could apply to any line(s) painted anywhere on the road to indicate the center of a two-way road, lane dividers on a highway, etc., rather than referring to the fog line at the right shoulder.

37. B: It is not true that the vehicle used in taking a road test is required to have turn signal indicators (b). If the vehicle does not have turn signals, the applicant being tested must use the designated hand signals. (In New York, some driving instructors have advocated the use of hand signals even when the turn signals work because the examiners supposedly "liked" this.) The applicant must provide the vehicle in which to take the road test (a). The DMV will not supply a test vehicle. The applicant also must produce proof of liability insurance (c) for the car used in the test, and this vehicle must pass a safety inspection (d) before being used in the test.

38. A: It is not correct that there is no accepted substitute for a valid registered license plate (a) on a car used to take a road test. If a car was recently purchased, for example, and the owner has not yet obtained the license plate(s) and/or registration, he may take the test after producing a bill of sale or other proof of purchase (b) within the past 30 days in lieu of the license plate(s)/registration. Taking the road test in a rented vehicle is permitted, as long as the applicant produces the rental contract and is listed on it as a driver of the vehicle (c). It also is correct that anyone taking the road test in a rented vehicle must show proof of insurance for that vehicle the same as for any other vehicle (d).

39. D: If weather makes conditions unsafe for the driver, the examiner, or both, a road test would not be given and would be rescheduled (d). However, an applicant would not have to wait any specified time period before rescheduling (c) and could schedule the next available appointment. The applicant would not go ahead and take the test anyway simply because unsafe weather conditions occur in real life (a). Licensed drivers should know when the weather makes driving conditions unsafe and refrain from driving in those conditions. By the same principle, the DMV will not administer a road test when the weather is unsafe for driving. The examiner would not go head and give the test but make allowances for the weather in scoring (b); the point is not that the weather is an unfair disadvantage to an applicant's performance and score, but that it is not safe to drive in inclement weather.

40. B: The road test does not normally include (b) parking within a parking lot. It normally does test parallel parking (a) in a single line of cars along a curb. It tests the ability to make a quick stop safely (c), i.e., going 20 mph and stopping as soon as the examiner says to do so. It also tests the applicant's ability to back the car for a distance (d), i.e., roughly 50 feet, going as straight and as smoothly as possible at a slow speed while looking behind the entire time.

41. A: Smooth accelerations (a) are not a part of the road test. While it is hoped an applicant knows how to increase speed smoothly rather than abruptly or jerkily--just as one knows how to stop quickly--this ability is not examined in the test. The road test does examine performance in stopping for traffic signs or lights (b) as well as at stop signs, pedestrian crosswalks, etc., and not proceeding until safe. It also tests performance of multi-point turns (c) in small spaces. (A three-point turn is sometimes called a "K-turn" from the K-shaped pattern it follows.) The road test also examines whether an applicant correctly yields the right of way (d) to pedestrians, bicyclists, and other drivers who enter an intersection first and whether the applicant stops and stays stopped until those with the right of way are out of the intersection.

42. D: The examiner in a road test will mark off points if an applicant does not get into the correct lane before arriving at a corner (a); if he does not use the turn signal light or hand signal far enough ahead of the corner (b) to notify those behind, or if the applicant does not look both ways before turning (c). When turning corners, drivers must do all of the above (d). All these elements are tested because they ensure greater safety when driving in real life. Failing to do (a) in real life not only could result in a ticket for an improper lane change but could cause an accident. The same is true for not signaling (b). Looking both left and right (c) is important to see if anything is coming and is especially important when turning where there are no traffic signal lights.

43. B: To avoid following too closely, it should take two seconds (b) to reach the same spot as the vehicle ahead. For example, when the car ahead passes something that can be used as a reference point, such as a power pole, a driver should be able to count "One-one-thousand, two-one-thousand" (or "one-Mississippi, two-Mississippi," etc.) before passing the same point. One second (a) is not long enough to prevent a driver from rear-ending the vehicle ahead if it brakes suddenly. Three seconds (c) and five seconds (d) are longer than needed and could require driving too slowly or braking unnecessarily to stay that far behind. In either case, another driver is likely to pass in between the two vehicles anyway.

44. C: An applicant who drives a car with a manual transmission (or stick shift) must demonstrate as a part of the road test that he can shift the gears correctly and smoothly (c). It is not true that the examiner must be certified to test drivers of manual transmissions (a). All examiners can test drivers of cars with either automatic or standard (manual) transmissions. It is not true that an applicant also must be tested driving an automatic transmission (b) if he drives a stick shift. Drivers only accustomed to automatic transmissions usually need some practice to learn to drive a standard shift, but those who learned on a stick shift generally do not need to learn new skills to drive an automatic transmission. It is not true that an applicant's driving is tested irrespective of how he handles the gearshift (d). Grinding the gears and lurching would not make a good impression on the examiner, and an applicant probably would not pass the road test.

45. D: Any of the choices given would have had a negative effect on Jack's score (d) on his road test. During the test--as during all driving--an applicant should keep both hands on the steering wheel. The examiner would take points off for a driver resting an elbow on the window and steering with only one hand (a). It is advised not to try to converse with the examiner (b), who will be occupied with giving instructions, taking notes, and writing down scores during the road test. Passing after checking behind his own vehicle only (c) would affect Jack's score because he did not check in front of his vehicle as well.

46. A: A vehicle must pass a safety inspection (a) before the road test for both commercial and non-commercial driver's licenses. For a commercial driver's license, the vehicle also must have a data plate showing the gross vehicle weight rating (GVWR), but road tests for non-commercial licenses do not require a weight rating. The minimum passing score (c) also can differ. For example, in Georgia the minimum passing score on the road test for a non-commercial driver's license is 75% while the minimum passing score for a commercial driver's license is 80%. Because only (a) does not differ but (b) and (c) differ between commercial and non-commercial license tests, answer (d), none of the above would differ, is incorrect.

47. C: A motorist may pass a motorcycle from an adjacent lane (c), either to the left or to the right of the motorcyclist's lane. It is not true that a motorist may pass it only on the left (a) or only on the right (b). More important, it is not true that a motorist may pass a motorcycle in the same lane if there is room (d). No matter how small the motorcycle, its driver or the passing car, motorcyclists legally are given the entire width of their lane, the same as a car. It is thus unlawful to be in the same lane as a motorcycle while passing it.

48. D: A solenoid cell (d) would not be involved if a vehicle has trouble stopping because it is not part of the car's brake system. It could be part of a car's starter circuit or fuel injection system, if the car has one. A master cylinder (a), a caliper(s) (b), and struts (c) all are parts of the automotive brake system. If something were wrong with any of these parts, a driver could have trouble stopping the vehicle, should not drive it, and should promptly take it to a mechanic.

49. B: The alternator (b) does not control exhaust emissions from the vehicle. It charges the car's battery and powers the car's electrical system while the engine is running. The catalytic converter (a) creates a chemical reaction that converts toxic exhaust byproducts to less toxic substances. After a number of years, it may need to be replaced for a vehicle to pass emissions inspection. If the inspection mechanic finds a hole in the car's exhaust pipe (c), for example, or something else wrong with the pipe, the car may fail the inspection until the pipe is replaced. An EGR—or Exhaust Gas Recirculation--valve (d), reduces nitrogen oxide emissions by recirculating part of the exhaust gas back into the car's cylinders, displacing some combustible material in the cylinders and reducing the heat of combustion, thereby reducing the amount of nitrogen oxide generated. If an emissions inspector says that a vehicle failed the "NOx test," the EGR valve may need to be replaced, if the car has one (not all cars do).

50. C: The Zone System (c) is not a method of safe or defensive driving. It is a photographic technique that allows photographers to systematically determine the optimum film exposure and development. The zone *control* system (d), on the other hand, is a driving strategy for keeping areas surrounding a vehicle clear to afford escape routes in case of an emergency. The SIPDE Process (a) stands for Sweep/Search/Scan; Identify hazards; Predict hazards, worst-case scenarios and possible actions; Decide on a safe action; and Execute the safe action. The SIPDE Process is often taught in driver education courses. The Smith System (b) was formulated by Harold K. Smith and is a system of safe and defensive driving similar to SIPDE that also has been used in driver education courses. It includes filmstrips Smith made demonstrating his system that teachers can show to their classes.

51. A: It is illegal (a) to flash the turn signal as a way of giving a following driver permission to pass. It is not a courtesy (b) because it is against the law, and therefore is not required by law (c) but prohibited. Because (a) is correct, answer (d), none of the above, is incorrect.

52. B: To parallel park correctly, a car should end up about (b) 18 inches away from the curb. To park 12 inches from the curb (a) would be expecting more precision from the driver than is usual or necessary, and would also increase the risk of hitting the curb. Twenty-four inches (c) away equals 2 feet, which is too far from the curb, putting the car in the way of street/road traffic, and 36 inches (d), which equals 3 feet, or 1 yard, away from the curb, puts the car in an even more precarious position.

53. D: The most accurate answer is (d): Eric is weaving, and it is against the law. A car on the highway is to pass other vehicles only after the driver has determined it is safe and has signaled the intended lane change. Constantly weaving to maintain a higher speed than the flow of traffic is illegal. Therefore Eric's driving is risky, but it is incorrect to say that it is not illegal (a) as well. Eric's driving also is inconsiderate, but it is not safe (b). Eric is a highly skilled driver of a car with superior handling, but these factors do not warrant weaving (c), which is unlawful.

54. A: A sign alerting motorists to temporary conditions such as highway construction or other road work would *not* be (a) a yellow diamond. It would be an orange diamond (b) or an orange rectangle (c). A yellow diamond (a) would be a sign warning motorists of permanent traffic patterns or conditions, not temporary ones. Because (b) and (c) fit the example description but (a) does not, answer (d), none of the above, is incorrect.

55. D: It is unlawful to stop, park, or stand on a sidewalk (a); in a crosswalk (b) on a street or road; or in an intersection (c) of roads or streets. A driver is never allowed to stop, stand, or park a motor vehicle on, at, or in any or all of the above (d). It also is unlawful to stop, park, or stand on the street side of a parked car; between a safety zone and the curb; along or across from any excavation or obstruction where one would block traffic by doing so; on an overpass, underpass, bridge, tunnel, or subway; on railroad tracks; on a controlled-access highway, and anywhere there is a No Parking sign.

56. B: A driver must be farthest away from (b) a railroad crossing if he has to stop, stand, or park a motor vehicle momentarily to pick up or drop off passengers. It is permissible by law to stop, stand, or park for a short time to pick up or drop off passengers at the places listed here at the following distances: At least 15 feet away from a fire hydrant (a); at least 20 feet away from a fire station's driveway (d); at least 30 feet away from a traffic control signal (c), a stop sign or a yield sign; and at least 50 feet away from a railroad crossing (b).

57. D: A driver should not make a U-turn (d) in any of these scenarios. If a sign says No U-turn (a) then U-turns are prohibited at that location and a driver could cause an accident as well as get a ticket for breaking the law. A driver should not make a U-turn on a curve in the road (b) because motorists coming from both directions cannot see the vehicle. Neither could drivers in either direction see a vehicle making a U-turn near the top of a hill (c), so U-turns should not be made there, either.

58. A: It is not true that speed limits are uniformly set by the federal government (a). They can be different in each state of the United States (c) because they are determined, posted, and enforced at the state level. Within each state the speed limits will differ depending on whether the location of the roads is urban, suburban, or rural (b). Because (a) is not correct but (b) and (c) are correct, answer (d), none of the above, is incorrect.

59. B: A driver should stop within 50 feet of the railroad crossing but not less than 15 feet from it. Therefore (b) is correct: A driver should be more than 15 feet away. It is not necessary to be more than 50 feet away (a). Because the rule is no less than 15 feet away, (c) is incorrect that a driver should be less than 15 feet away, and it follows that at least 10 feet away (d) is not far enough for safety, either.

60. C: A driver must always stop at a railroad crossing when (c) either of these is true: The crossing gates are lowered (a) and/or the railroad signal is flashing (b). Therefore answer (d), that it is always required to stop when neither of the above is the case, is incorrect.

61. D: At a railroad crossing, if a flagman is giving a signal (a) to stop, drivers must always stop; and/or if the train itself is giving a warning signal (b), drivers must always stop as well. Therefore the correct answer is that each of the above always means cars must stop (d) before a railroad crossing: Answer (c), neither of the above, is incorrect.

62. C: It is not true that (c) two-thirds of all road workers are killed by motor vehicles in work zones. It is true that more than half of all road workers' deaths are caused by motor vehicles (a). It is also true that of these deaths by motor vehicles, one-third are caused by the vehicles intruding into the work zones (b). As (c) is not true but (a) and (b) are true, answer (d), none of these statements is true, is incorrect.

63. D: Work zones include not only construction or maintenance work on roads themselves but areas where people are working on overhead power lines (a); areas where workers are operating snow plows or otherwise working to remove snow from the roads (b); and areas where surveyors are measuring land near the roads (c), which can sometimes also involve their entering the roads. Therefore, the correct answer is (d) all of the above are defined as work zones.

64. B: The incorrect statement is (b), speed limits are always slower than the usual in work zones. Speed limits very often are lowered for safety, but they also may be the same as usually posted (a). A driver who violates the posted speed limit in a work zone can be fined (c); for example, in Georgia the fine is more than $100 and less than $2,000. Moreover, a driver breaking a work zone speed limit can be imprisoned (d) for up to a year, or can be both fined and imprisoned for the violation.

65. C: It is not a valid tip that it is not necessary to slow down when entering a road work zone (c). Most manuals advise drivers to slow down when entering a work zone. They also advise drivers to try to move into a lane farther away from the work (a) if they are in a lane nearer to the work. Another good tip is to expect and prepare for the unexpected in a road work zone (b). Manuals also advise drivers to pay attention to the posted speed limits in any work zone, not only because they may be different, but because, in most work zones, the fines for breaking these speed limits are higher (d) than elsewhere on highways or roads.

66. C: The true statement is that (c) a driver who is 21 years of age or older is classified as intoxicated if his blood alcohol is greater than 0.08 percent by weight. Although a driver may have impaired driving ability at a lower level such as 0.02 percent (a, b), this is not the definition of driving while intoxicated. Additionally, many states will prosecute drivers under the age of 21 if there is any detectable amount of alcohol in their system (d), even though they are not strictly intoxicated, since the law prohibits the sale of alcohol to minors.

67. A: It is true that (a) having a prescription for a drug does not constitute a defense if that drug impairs the driver's ability to operate a motor vehicle safely, whether the drug impairs the driver's judgment, physical reflexes, reaction times or coordination. It is not true that the laws are the same for illegal drugs and alcohol but different for legal drugs (b). Neither is it true that driving under the influence of legal and illegal drugs is governed by laws different from those for driving under the influence of alcohol (c). Further, it is not true that the laws regarding driving under the influence no longer apply if a driver is prescribed a drug necessary for health (d). If a prescription drug is required to maintain a person's health and the drug impairs the person's ability to drive safely, then that person should not drive under the influence of that drug. If the person is always under the influence of a drug that impairs his ability to drive, then that person cannot drive.

68. D: Aggressive driving is considered operating a motor vehicle with the intent to (d) do any of these: (a) annoy, harass, (b) molest, intimidate, or (c) injure or obstruct another person in any way.

69. C: The penalty for aggressive driving that applies specifically to drivers under 21 years of age is (c) suspension of all driving privileges. Punishment by fine (a) or by imprisonment (b) applies to drivers of all ages if they are convicted. However, only those under 21 will incur suspension of driving privileges if convicted of aggressive driving.

70. B: It is not true that reckless driving is the same as aggressive driving (b). Reckless driving is defined as driving any motor vehicle with reckless disregard for the safety of persons or property. Penalties for driving recklessly include being fined (a); being imprisoned (c), and, for drivers under age 21, the suspension of all driving privileges (d). Note that while the definitions of aggressive driving and reckless driving differ, the penalties are the same.

71. A: The correct statement is (a): The distance for following any moving emergency vehicle or apparatus, such as a fire truck, is 200 feet or more. It is not correct to park at a distance of 200 feet from stopped emergency vehicles or apparatus (b). The law requires parking 500 feet or more away from any emergency vehicles or apparatus that are stopped in response to a fire alarm. Because the distance of 200 feet or more is correct for following emergency vehicles or apparatus responding to a fire alarm when they are in motion, a distance of 500 feet or more for following (c) is incorrect. Because (a) is correct, answer (d), none of the above, is incorrect.

72. C: The *most* accurate statement is (c): It is against the law for vehicles pulling trailers to engage in "caravanning." In other words, cars or trucks pulling trailers should not form a "caravan" with other vehicles pulling trailers. The law states that vehicles with trailers must leave enough space between their trailer and other vehicles with trailers so another vehicle could safely enter the lane behind or in front of them; therefore, it is untrue that (d) it is unnecessary to leave space for other vehicles if pulling a trailer. It also is untrue that caravanning by vehicles with trailers is encouraged (a). While it is true that this practice is discouraged (b), this is not the *most* accurate answer because not only is caravanning discouraged but is actually illegal (c).

73. B: It is not true that the laws differ for riding in house trailers or horse trailers (b). The law is the same for riding in any trailer drawn by a vehicle (as opposed to a motor vehicle trailer built to be driven, not pulled). It is against the law to ride in a trailer drawn by a vehicle (a). This is because riders in such trailers do not have the benefit of restraints as do vehicle riders with seat belts (c) and air bags. It also is because separation of the trailer from the vehicle would pose a distinct hazard to riders (d) in the event that the trailer hitch or other connector was broken.

74. C: It is not true that wearing a hands-free Bluetooth device (c) in the ear is allowed while driving a motor vehicle. (Hands-free devices not in the ear or on the head, such as speaker phones, are permitted, as is playing music in the vehicle, with the proviso that the volume is not so loud as to obscure traffic sounds.) It is illegal in some states to use a hand-held cell phone while driving (a), although it is not illegal in every state. It is illegal to wear headsets, headphones (d), or anything that can interfere with a person's hearing (b) while driving. This applies to earphones or headphones for listening to music as well as those used for telephone conversations, or for listening to anything that could override the sounds occurring outside of one's earphones or headphones.

75. A: Wearing glasses or contact lenses--assuming such correction is necessary and prescribed--even though not specified on a driver's license (a) is less likely to violate a law than the other choices here. If a driver requires corrective lenses to pass the initial vision screening, a restriction for corrective lenses will be placed on the license, so the absence of such information on the license is not likely. Also, vision information is updated whenever one must renew his license or has a transaction with the DMV. If status regarding vision correction has changed, a driver either must take another vision screening or submit a current form (e.g., DS-274) to verify visual status. Driving with another person or an animal on one's lap (b) could violate a law regarding obstruction of view and/or interfering with mechanical operation of the vehicle. Wearing sunglasses at night or in the dark (c) also would impair vision while driving. Driving a car piled full of objects (d) could obstruct the ability to see all around the vehicle (ahead of, behind, and to the sides). Driving under such conditions and/or anything else that interferes with one's view is against the law.

76. D: In North America, Australia, and New Zealand, a school zone sign (d) would not be red with white but would be yellow with black, which is the color scheme used on warning signs in these countries. In the United States, fluorescent green also may be used on warning signs instead of yellow. Stop signs (a), yield signs (b), and signs forbidding certain actions, such as parking (c), all use a color scheme of red with white in these countries.

77. C: Road signs and markers are standardized on federal highways (c) in the United States. They are not standardized, and can vary, on local roads (a); among county markers (b); and on state highways (d).

78. D: This color scheme is used for all the choices given (d). In the United States, orange signs with black letters and/or symbols are used to indicate detours (a); road construction (b); and zones where traffic is under temporary control (c), such as for road work, construction, or special events.

79. A: In the United States, green signs with white are not used for (a) historical sites. Signs to historical sites are brown with white. Green signs with white are used to designate places (b); distances, i.e., how many miles to a particular location (c), and to give directions (d).

80. B: Signs to campgrounds in the United States use (b) brown with white color schemes. Blue with white (a) signs indicate services, such as food/gas/lodging. White with black (c) is used for regulatory signs, such as speed limits or parking. Yellow with black (d) signs are for warnings, such as school zones or curves.

81. C: In the United States, a brown with white sign would not indicate (c) a rest are(a) A rest area would be indicated by a blue with white sign, as would other services, such as hospitals or food/gas/lodging. In the United States, brown signs with white letters designate parks (a), ski areas (b), and forests (d), as well as campgrounds and historical sites.

82. A: In the United States, a stop sign has (a) eight sides, i.e., it is an octagon. It does not have six (b) sides which would make it a hexagon. Neither does it have four (c) sides, which would make it a diamond, a rectangle, or a square. Diamond-shaped signs are for warnings. Vertical rectangles are used for service signs, speed limit signs, etc., and horizontal rectangles are used for directional signs. The stop sign does not have three (d) sides, which would be a triangle. Yield signs are triangular.

83. B: A pentagonal sign, or a sign with five sides, is likely to show (b) a school crossing. It is also used to designate a school zone. It normally has a black silhouette of a boy and girl crossing the street. A hazard warning (a) would be a diamond-shaped sign. A railroad crossing (c) is indicated by a round sign. Signs indicating the need to yield (d) the right of way are triangular.

84. B: Kangaroo crossing signs in Australia are (b) diamond-shaped because they indicate a warning. The same shape rules apply in Australia and the United States. A round (a) sign would indicate a railroad crossing. A triangular (c) sign would be a sign to yield the right of way. A rectangular (d) sign if vertical could indicate services, speed limits, etc.; if horizontal, it could indicate directions, street and place names and such.

85. B: A Thru Traffic sign would be (b) a horizontal rectangle because it gives directions to motorists. Signs with this shape generally are guide signs that indicate locations, directions, or other information to help guide the driver. A vertical rectangle (a) more likely would be a regulatory sign, such as No Parking or a speed limit sign. A diamond shape (c) is associated with warning signs. A triangular shape (d) is associated with yield signs.

86. A: A vertically rectangular white sign with No Parking in red or black letters (a) must be obeyed the same way that traffic laws are obeyed. It is not merely a suggestion (b) but a law. The sign must be obeyed whether the lettering is in red or black (c). The legality of such regulatory signs does not vary from one place to another (d) but is standard in the United States.

87. C: Purple is used only (c) to indicate toll lanes designated for vehicles with registered electronic toll collection (ETC) accounts. Drivers of these vehicles have registered an account to have their tolls collected electronically. To promote more efficient traffic flow, such vehicles will be directed to lanes separate from those where cash is used to pay toll fees. Signs indicating the lanes for ECT are purple in the United States. Therefore it is not true that there is no such thing as a purple road sign in this country. (a). Purple is not sometimes used on incident management signs (b), but these signs may be fluorescent pink, according to the US Manual on Uniform Traffic Control Devices. Purple is never used on detour signs (d), not even as a nonstandard color.

88. B: It is not true that (b) all road signs in the US use the English language only. Signs near the US-Mexico border frequently are bilingual, using both Spanish and English. Some bilingual signs with French and English also may be found in the United States, for example, in parts of Vermont or Louisiana. It is true that road signs in the United States and Canada may have one, two, or three languages (a). For example, Mistissini, a town in Québec in Canada, has signs with English, French, and Cree, a Native American language, as the citizens may speak any of these three languages. It is true that certain locations in both Canada and the United States have bilingual French/English or English/French road signs (c). It is true that most of Canada uses English signs but has French signs in Québec (d), a province with a historically large French-speaking population. As seen above, some places in Canada have multilingual signs in addition to the mostly English signs used throughout the country and the French signs mostly used in Québec.

89. D: In Israel, many road signs are in (d) all three of the languages listed: Hebrew (a) because the majority of the population is made up of Israeli Jews whose first language is Hebrew; Arabic (b) because much of the population in Israel is made up of Arab peoples such as Palestinians, Arabians, Egyptians, etc., who speak Arabic, and English (c) because many people in Israel are Jews who migrated from English-speaking countries as well as other English-speaking people who live there, and because English is taught and spoken in so many foreign countries today for diplomatic, economic, and educational reasons.

90. C: Fluorescent yellow (c) is not an alternative color used today for road signs in many parts of the United States. Fluorescent pink (a) may be used on signs at incident management sites instead of the traditional orange used for temporary traffic control zones. Fluorescent green (b) may be used instead of yellow for warning signs indicating school zones, school bus stops, playgrounds, pedestrians, and bicyclists. Fluorescent orange (d) often is used in the United States and Canada instead of non-fluorescent orange to indicate construction sites or zones.

91. B: A sign saying (b) Two-Way Traffic is not classified as a regulatory sign but as a warning sign. It is a yellow diamond with black symbols and letters. The purpose of this sign is to warn motorists that a separated one-way highway is about to end and they will be entering a highway with two-way traffic. Regulatory signs are rectangular and tell drivers what they can or cannot do. A sign saying (a) Do Not Enter typically will be a square white sign with a red circle, a white horizontal bar across the center of the red circle, and white letters, indicating a one-way road that must not be entered from the direction one is traveling. A sign saying (c) Wrong Way is typically a red horizontal rectangle with white letters and indicates that a driver is approaching a one-way highway or highway ramp. A sign saying (d) One Way typically is a white vertical rectangle with black letters and a black arrow pointing either left or right to indicate travel is allowed only in that one direction on the road where the sign is posted.

92. A: What is true about hydroplaning is that (a) drivers cannot brake, accelerate, or steer if they are doing it. Hydroplaning means that when driving on a road with standing water on it, a vehicle's tires may actually lose contact with the road and skim along the surface of the water as speed increases. Traction is the friction between wheels or tires and the ground that allows a vehicle to move forward. There is less friction, or traction, on a wet road than on a dry road surface. Without traction, it is impossible to brake to stop or slow the car, to use the accelerator to speed up, or to use the steering wheel to change direction. Obviously this is very dangerous. Hydroplaning can occur at speeds as low as 35 mph with standard passenger cars, which is why it is important to drive more slowly when it is raining and/or there is water on the road. Hydroplaning is not plowing through standing water with the car tires still on the road (b). It occurs when the tires lose contact with the road surface. At speeds below 35 mph, cars typically do plow through standing water as the tires will push the water away at lower speeds, similar to the way windshield wipers do. Hydroplaning is not defined as operating an airplane atop or above the water (c) even though the word sounds as if this could be a plausible definition. Neither does it mean driving on a plane or surface that is under deep water (d), which is not possible with most motor vehicles.

93. D: If a driver goes into a skid, he should (d) steer the car in the direction of the skid, not away from it (c) as is many people's first reaction if they have not learned otherwise. Trying to steer away from the skid will only make it worse. Steering into the skid can minimize sliding by moving the tires back into a position with more potential traction, whereas turning them away creates more skidding surface on the tires. Slippery road surfaces exaggerate all movements, so no maneuvers should be sharp or sudden. One should ease one's foot off the gas pedal, not yank it off (a) abruptly. One should never stomp on the brakes (b) as this will stop the wheels from turning and all they can do then is continue to skid. A driver should only lightly apply brakes and steer in a safe direction after recovering control of the vehicle, i.e., when it is no longer skidding.

94. A: Answer (a) does not correctly complete this statement: Generally, it can take up to 100 feet to stop a vehicle from a speed of *20* mph, not 30 mph as stated in choice (a). Generally it does take up to 200 feet to stop a vehicle going 40 mph (b); up to 400 feet to stop from a speed of 60 mph (c), and up to 600 feet to stop a vehicle going 80 mph. Such increases in stopping distances are why it is so important not to exceed the speed limit in case an emergency requires stopping unexpectedly. Many accidents are caused when drivers are going too fast to stop in the distance available. In addition to laws of physics, which govern how far a vehicle will travel before completely stopping from various speeds, other factors affecting stopping times and distances must be taken into account. These include the driver's mental and physical reaction time; the type of pavement and its condition; the type of tires and the composition of their treads; the design of the vehicle's chassis (or frame); the kind of brakes, their balance and condition, and the direction and velocity of any wind.

95. B: It is not true that the chances of pedestrian fatality are less than 60% if struck by a vehicle going 40 mph (b). If a vehicle going 40 mph strikes a pedestrian, the chances the pedestrian will die are actually *80%*. Therefore, it is true that the chances of fatality are more than 70% at this speed (d). It is also true that the chances of pedestrian mortality are less than 10% if the vehicle was going 20 mph (a), and that if a vehicle going 30 mph strikes a pedestrian, the chances the pedestrian will die are less than 50% (c).

96. C: Where there is a median strip between roads or opposing lanes of roads, only authorized openings, turnarounds, or crossovers may be used (c) to go to the other side of the median. It is not only frowned on but illegal to drive across the median (a). There is no provision in the law for driving on a median in emergencies (b). It is not specifically encouraged to use the median strip to avoid a collision (d).

97. B: In the situation described, the law states that (b) it would be the fault of the person who opened the car door into traffic. The law prohibits opening the doors of vehicles on the traffic side unless it is safe to do so and will not interfere with the movement of traffic. Therefore, it would not be the fault of the moving vehicle's driver (a). It would not be necessary for a police officer or judge to determine fault (c) because the law is clear. Because the law prohibits opening vehicle doors into traffic if it is unsafe or interferes with traffic, fault would not lie equally with both the opener of the door and the driver of the vehicle that hit the door (d).

98. D: The statement that is not true is (d). It is permitted for a traffic control device to direct drivers the opposite way on a one-way street; therefore, it is not illegal to do so. In addition to traffic control devices, other conditions that permit driving the wrong way on a one-way street are if (a): it is necessary for police vehicles to do so; (b): if it is necessary for authorized emergency vehicles, and (c): if authorized construction or emergency workers direct drivers to do so.

99. B: A sign saying Keep Right (b) is not a warning sign but a regulatory sign. Such a sign will typically be a white vertical rectangle with black letters and symbols, often showing a shape with an arrow going around it to the right. It directs motorists to stay to the right to go around medians or obstructions in the road. A sign saying Merge (a) is a warning sign and will be a yellow diamond with black letters and arrows showing that traffic will be merging from the right or the left, alerting motorists to prepare to allow traffic to merge safely. A sign saying Signal Ahead (c) is a warning sign that is often a yellow diamond with a picture of a traffic signal light and a smaller yellow rectangle below the diamond with the words Signal Ahead. This sign is to alert motorists that a traffic signal is ahead and they should slow down and prepare to stop. This sign is often used where the signal is not visible from a distance, as with hills and curves. No Passing Zone (d) is a warning sign and will be yellow. It often is triangular and is posted on the left side of a highway to alert motorists that they are entering a zone where no passing is allowed.

100. C: The standard position of the green light on a traffic signal is (c) on the bottom. It is not on the top (a), which is where the red light is located. It is not in the middle (b), where the yellow light is located. It is not true that there is no standard (d) for the positioning of lights. The positions are standardized to prevent confusion for motorists. Drivers with red-green colorblindness also benefit from this standard. Though they may have vision restrictions on their licenses, they can still identify the lights to stop and go from their uniform positioning. The red light is on the top, the more prominent position, because there are more situations in which it is safer to stop than to go and, conversely, more situations in which it is more dangerous to go than to stop.

How to Overcome Test Anxiety

Just the thought of taking a test is enough to make most people a little nervous. A test is an important event that can have a long-term impact on your future, so it's important to take it seriously and it's natural to feel anxious about performing well. But just because anxiety is normal, that doesn't mean that it's helpful in test taking, or that you should simply accept it as part of your life. Anxiety can have a variety of effects. These effects can be mild, like making you feel slightly nervous, or severe, like blocking your ability to focus or remember even a simple detail.

If you experience test anxiety—whether severe or mild—it's important to know how to beat it. To discover this, first you need to understand what causes test anxiety.

Causes of Test Anxiety

While we often think of anxiety as an uncontrollable emotional state, it can actually be caused by simple, practical things. One of the most common causes of test anxiety is that a person does not feel adequately prepared for their test. This feeling can be the result of many different issues such as poor study habits or lack of organization, but the most common culprit is time management. Starting to study too late, failing to organize your study time to cover all of the material, or being distracted while you study will mean that you're not well prepared for the test. This may lead to cramming the night before, which will cause you to be physically and mentally exhausted for the test. Poor time management also contributes to feelings of stress, fear, and hopelessness as you realize you are not well prepared but don't know what to do about it.

Other times, test anxiety is not related to your preparation for the test but comes from unresolved fear. This may be a past failure on a test, or poor performance on tests in general. It may come from comparing yourself to others who seem to be performing better or from the stress of living up to expectations. Anxiety may be driven by fears of the future—how failure on this test would affect your educational and career goals. These fears are often completely irrational, but they can still negatively impact your test performance.

Elements of Test Anxiety

As mentioned earlier, test anxiety is considered to be an emotional state, but it has physical and mental components as well. Sometimes you may not even realize that you are suffering from test anxiety until you notice the physical symptoms. These can include trembling hands, rapid heartbeat, sweating, nausea, and tense muscles. Extreme anxiety may lead to fainting or vomiting. Obviously, any of these symptoms can have a negative impact on testing. It is important to recognize them as soon as they begin to occur so that you can address the problem before it damages your performance.

The mental components of test anxiety include trouble focusing and inability to remember learned information. During a test, your mind is on high alert, which can help you recall information and stay focused for an extended period of time. However, anxiety interferes with your mind's natural processes, causing you to blank out, even on the questions you know well. The strain of testing during anxiety makes it difficult to stay focused, especially on a test that may take several hours. Extreme anxiety can take a huge mental toll, making it difficult not only to recall test information but even to understand the test questions or pull your thoughts together.

Effects of Test Anxiety

Test anxiety is like a disease—if left untreated, it will get progressively worse. Anxiety leads to poor performance, and this reinforces the feelings of fear and failure, which in turn lead to poor performances on subsequent tests. It can grow from a mild nervousness to a crippling condition. If allowed to progress, test anxiety can have a big impact on your schooling, and consequently on your future.

Test anxiety can spread to other parts of your life. Anxiety on tests can become anxiety in any stressful situation, and blanking on a test can turn into panicking in a job situation. But fortunately, you don't have to let anxiety rule your testing and determine your grades. There are a number of relatively simple steps you can take to move past anxiety and function normally on a test and in the rest of life.

Physical Steps for Beating Test Anxiety

While test anxiety is a serious problem, the good news is that it can be overcome. It doesn't have to control your ability to think and remember information. While it may take time, you can begin taking steps today to beat anxiety.

Just as your first hint that you may be struggling with anxiety comes from the physical symptoms, the first step to treating it is also physical. Rest is crucial for having a clear, strong mind. If you are tired, it is much easier to give in to anxiety. But if you establish good sleep habits, your body and mind will be ready to perform optimally, without the strain of exhaustion. Additionally, sleeping well helps you to retain information better, so you're more likely to recall the answers when you see the test questions.

Getting good sleep means more than going to bed on time. It's important to allow your brain time to relax. Take study breaks from time to time so it doesn't get overworked, and don't study right before bed. Take time to rest your mind before trying to rest your body, or you may find it difficult to fall asleep.

Along with sleep, other aspects of physical health are important in preparing for a test. Good nutrition is vital for good brain function. Sugary foods and drinks may give a burst of energy but this burst is followed by a crash, both physically and emotionally. Instead, fuel your body with protein and vitamin-rich foods.

Also, drink plenty of water. Dehydration can lead to headaches and exhaustion, especially if your brain is already under stress from the rigors of the test. Particularly if your test is a long one, drink water during the breaks. And if possible, take an energy-boosting snack to eat between sections.

Along with sleep and diet, a third important part of physical health is exercise. Maintaining a steady workout schedule is helpful, but even taking 5-minute study breaks to walk can help get your blood pumping faster and clear your head. Exercise also releases endorphins, which contribute to a positive feeling and can help combat test anxiety.

When you nurture your physical health, you are also contributing to your mental health. If your body is healthy, your mind is much more likely to be healthy as well. So take time to rest, nourish your body with healthy food and water, and get moving as much as possible. Taking these physical steps will make you stronger and more able to take the mental steps necessary to overcome test anxiety.

Mental Steps for Beating Test Anxiety

Working on the mental side of test anxiety can be more challenging, but as with the physical side, there are clear steps you can take to overcome it. As mentioned earlier, test anxiety often stems from lack of preparation, so the obvious solution is to prepare for the test. Effective studying may be the most important weapon you have for beating test anxiety, but you can and should employ several other mental tools to combat fear.

First, boost your confidence by reminding yourself of past success—tests or projects that you aced. If you're putting as much effort into preparing for this test as you did for those, there's no reason you should expect to fail here. Work hard to prepare; then trust your preparation.

Second, surround yourself with encouraging people. It can be helpful to find a study group, but be sure that the people you're around will encourage a positive attitude. If you spend time with others who are anxious or cynical, this will only contribute to your own anxiety. Look for others who are motivated to study hard from a desire to succeed, not from a fear of failure.

Third, reward yourself. A test is physically and mentally tiring, even without anxiety, and it can be helpful to have something to look forward to. Plan an activity following the test, regardless of the outcome, such as going to a movie or getting ice cream.

When you are taking the test, if you find yourself beginning to feel anxious, remind yourself that you know the material. Visualize successfully completing the test. Then take a few deep, relaxing breaths and return to it. Work through the questions carefully but with confidence, knowing that you are capable of succeeding.

Developing a healthy mental approach to test taking will also aid in other areas of life. Test anxiety affects more than just the actual test—it can be damaging to your mental health and even contribute to depression. It's important to beat test anxiety before it becomes a problem for more than testing.

Study Strategy

Being prepared for the test is necessary to combat anxiety, but what does being prepared look like? You may study for hours on end and still not feel prepared. What you need is a strategy for test prep. The next few pages outline our recommended steps to help you plan out and conquer the challenge of preparation.

Step 1: Scope Out the Test

Learn everything you can about the format (multiple choice, essay, etc.) and what will be on the test. Gather any study materials, course outlines, or sample exams that may be available. Not only will this help you to prepare, but knowing what to expect can help to alleviate test anxiety.

Step 2: Map Out the Material

Look through the textbook or study guide and make note of how many chapters or sections it has. Then divide these over the time you have. For example, if a book has 15 chapters and you have five days to study, you need to cover three chapters each day. Even better, if you have the time, leave an extra day at the end for overall review after you have gone through the material in depth.

If time is limited, you may need to prioritize the material. Look through it and make note of which sections you think you already have a good grasp on, and which need review. While you are studying, skim quickly through the familiar sections and take more time on the challenging parts.

Write out your plan so you don't get lost as you go. Having a written plan also helps you feel more in control of the study, so anxiety is less likely to arise from feeling overwhelmed at the amount to cover.

Step 3: Gather Your Tools

Decide what study method works best for you. Do you prefer to highlight in the book as you study and then go back over the highlighted portions? Or do you type out notes of the important information? Or is it helpful to make flashcards that you can carry with you? Assemble the pens, index cards, highlighters, post-it notes, and any other materials you may need so you won't be distracted by getting up to find things while you study.

If you're having a hard time retaining the information or organizing your notes, experiment with different methods. For example, try color-coding by subject with colored pens, highlighters, or post-it notes. If you learn better by hearing, try recording yourself reading your notes so you can listen while in the car, working out, or simply sitting at your desk. Ask a friend to quiz you from your flashcards, or try teaching someone the material to solidify it in your mind.

Step 4: Create Your Environment

It's important to avoid distractions while you study. This includes both the obvious distractions like visitors and the subtle distractions like an uncomfortable chair (or a too-comfortable couch that makes you want to fall asleep). Set up the best study environment possible: good lighting and a comfortable work area. If background music helps you focus, you may want to turn it on, but otherwise keep the room quiet. If you are using a computer to take notes, be sure you don't have any other windows open, especially applications like social media, games, or anything else that could distract you. Silence your phone and turn off notifications. Be sure to keep water close by so you stay hydrated while you study (but avoid unhealthy drinks and snacks).

Also, take into account the best time of day to study. Are you freshest first thing in the morning? Try to set aside some time then to work through the material. Is your mind clearer in the afternoon or evening? Schedule your study session then. Another method is to study at the same time of day that you will take the test, so that your brain gets used to working on the material at that time and will be ready to focus at test time.

Step 5: Study!

Once you have done all the study preparation, it's time to settle into the actual studying. Sit down, take a few moments to settle your mind so you can focus, and begin to follow your study plan. Don't give in to distractions or let yourself procrastinate. This is your time to prepare so you'll be ready to fearlessly approach the test. Make the most of the time and stay focused.

Of course, you don't want to burn out. If you study too long you may find that you're not retaining the information very well. Take regular study breaks. For example, taking five minutes out of every hour to walk briskly, breathing deeply and swinging your arms, can help your mind stay fresh.

As you get to the end of each chapter or section, it's a good idea to do a quick review. Remind yourself of what you learned and work on any difficult parts. When you feel that you've mastered the material, move on to the next part. At the end of your study session, briefly skim through your notes again.

But while review is helpful, cramming last minute is NOT. If at all possible, work ahead so that you won't need to fit all your study into the last day. Cramming overloads your brain with more information than it can process and retain, and your tired mind may struggle to recall even previously learned information when it is overwhelmed with last-minute study. Also, the urgent nature of cramming and the stress placed on your brain contribute to anxiety. You'll be more likely to go to the test feeling unprepared and having trouble thinking clearly.

So don't cram, and don't stay up late before the test, even just to review your notes at a leisurely pace. Your brain needs rest more than it needs to go over the information again. In fact, plan to finish your studies by noon or early afternoon the day before the test. Give your brain the rest of the day to relax or focus on other things, and get a good night's sleep. Then you will be fresh for the test and better able to recall what you've studied.

Step 6: Take a Practice Test

Many courses offer sample tests, either online or in the study materials. This is an excellent resource to check whether you have mastered the material, as well as to prepare for the test format and environment.

Check the test format ahead of time: the number of questions, the type (multiple choice, free response, etc.), and the time limit. Then create a plan for working through them. For example, if you have 30 minutes to take a 60-question test, your limit is 30 seconds per question. Spend less time on the questions you know well so that you can take more time on the difficult ones.

If you have time to take several practice tests, take the first one open book, with no time limit. Work through the questions at your own pace and make sure you fully understand them. Gradually work up to taking a test under test conditions: sit at a desk with all study materials put away and set a timer. Pace yourself to make sure you finish the test with time to spare and go back to check your answers if you have time.

After each test, check your answers. On the questions you missed, be sure you understand why you missed them. Did you misread the question (tests can use tricky wording)? Did you forget the information? Or was it something you hadn't learned? Go back and study any shaky areas that the practice tests reveal.

Taking these tests not only helps with your grade, but also aids in combating test anxiety. If you're already used to the test conditions, you're less likely to worry about it, and working through tests until you're scoring well gives you a confidence boost. Go through the practice tests until you feel comfortable, and then you can go into the test knowing that you're ready for it.

Test Tips

On test day, you should be confident, knowing that you've prepared well and are ready to answer the questions. But aside from preparation, there are several test day strategies you can employ to maximize your performance.

First, as stated before, get a good night's sleep the night before the test (and for several nights before that, if possible). Go into the test with a fresh, alert mind rather than staying up late to study.

Try not to change too much about your normal routine on the day of the test. It's important to eat a nutritious breakfast, but if you normally don't eat breakfast at all, consider eating just a protein bar. If you're a coffee drinker, go ahead and have your normal coffee. Just make sure you time it so that the caffeine doesn't wear off right in the middle of your test. Avoid sugary beverages, and drink enough water to stay hydrated but not so much that you need a restroom break 10 minutes into the test. If your test isn't first thing in the morning, consider going for a walk or doing a light workout before the test to get your blood flowing.

Allow yourself enough time to get ready, and leave for the test with plenty of time to spare so you won't have the anxiety of scrambling to arrive in time. Another reason to be early is to select a good seat. It's helpful to sit away from doors and windows, which can be distracting. Find a good seat, get out your supplies, and settle your mind before the test begins.

When the test begins, start by going over the instructions carefully, even if you already know what to expect. Make sure you avoid any careless mistakes by following the directions.

Then begin working through the questions, pacing yourself as you've practiced. If you're not sure on an answer, don't spend too much time on it, and don't let it shake your confidence. Either skip it and come back later, or eliminate as many wrong answers as possible and guess among the remaining ones. Don't dwell on these questions as you continue—put them out of your mind and focus on what lies ahead.

Be sure to read all of the answer choices, even if you're sure the first one is the right answer. Sometimes you'll find a better one if you keep reading. But don't second-guess yourself if you do immediately know the answer. Your gut instinct is usually right. Don't let test anxiety rob you of the information you know.

If you have time at the end of the test (and if the test format allows), go back and review your answers. Be cautious about changing any, since your first instinct tends to be correct, but make sure you didn't misread any of the questions or accidentally mark the wrong answer choice. Look over any you skipped and make an educated guess.

At the end, leave the test feeling confident. You've done your best, so don't waste time worrying about your performance or wishing you could change anything. Instead, celebrate the successful completion of this test. And finally, use this test to learn how to deal with anxiety even better next time.

Review Video: Test Anxiety
Visit mometrix.com/academy and enter code: 100340

Important Qualification

Not all anxiety is created equal. If your test anxiety is causing major issues in your life beyond the classroom or testing center, or if you are experiencing troubling physical symptoms related to your anxiety, it may be a sign of a serious physiological or psychological condition. If this sounds like your situation, we strongly encourage you to seek professional help.

Online Resources

Due to our efforts to try to keep this book to a manageable length, we've created a link that will give you access to all of your online resources:

mometrix.com/resources719/priisafdrived

It's Your Moment, Let's Celebrate It!

Share your story @mometrixtestpreparation